Guide to Trapping

JIM SPENCER

STACKPOLE BOOKS

0 11557 03417 2

To Jill.
No one who knows her will need to ask why.

Published by
STACKPOLE BOOKS
5067 Ritter Road
Mechanicsburg, PA 17055
www.stackpolebooks.com

Printed in the United States

First edition

10 9 8 7 6 5 4 3 2 1

Cover photographs by Bill Bradbury, Jill Easton, and Jim Spencer
Cover design by Wendy Reynolds

Photos by author except on the following pages: Jill Easton: 5, 7, 24, 25, 30, 31, 35, 58,
60, 62, 68, 72, 73, 74, 77, 82, 88, 91, 133, 155 (top), 162, 169, 175, 177, 179, 181, 191,
196; Bill Bradbury: 120, 188; Robin Goff: 13; Keith Sutton: 16, 38, 48, 69, 101, 106,
172, 186; Bill McGhee: 155 (bottom); U.S. Fish and Wildlife Service: 97, 139 (top); Ken
Fanning: 123, 170, 182; Linda Bradbury: 184; Harold McAlpine: 164

Illustrations by Caroline Stover

Library of Congress Cataloging-in-Publication Data
Spencer, Jim, 1947-
  Guide to trapping / Jim Spencer.—1st ed.
      p. cm.
  Includes index.
  ISBN-13: 978-0-8117-3417-2
  ISBN-10: 0-8117-3417-X
  1. Trapping. I. Title.

SK283.S56 2007
639'.1—dc22

2006038366

Contents

Foreword

I've known Jim Spencer a long, long time. Exactly when and where we first met, I can't remember. A lot of water has gone under both our bridges since then, some of it flavored with the bourbon we've shared around hundreds of campfires. I do know that when we met, neither of us had gray in our beards, and that was eons ago.

The reason we met, though, is clear and certain. Both of us are hook-and-bullet writers, which makes both of us strange birds, and strange birds tend to flock together. We both live in Arkansas—always have—so it was inevitable our paths would cross.

Actually, our paths didn't cross; they merged. In the 1980s, we both were hired by the state's natural resources agency as writers and public-relations types, and during most of our almost twenty-year tenure there, we worked together writing and editing the agency's conservation magazine. Everything Jim wrote, I edited, and everything I wrote, Jim edited. We also edited scores of articles by other writers. We often spent days brainstorming about the proper way to tackle a conservation-related issue of importance, and though we butted heads about as often as we agreed, in the end, we produced a magazine both of us will always be proud of.

I tell you these things so you'll know why I'm qualified to enlighten you about the man whose words you are about to read. I can read a single sentence Jim has written and know immediately the words are his. His style is that unique. And I can say without hesitation that very few outdoor writers possess his skill for wordsmithing. The sentences he crafts define us as outdoorsmen. They are magical and unforgettable and insightful all at once. When you read Jim Spencer, you are certain to become a Jim Spencer fan.

I also can tell you that no man ever loved trapping more than Jim. When I first went with him to run one of his lines, I was astounded. The 200-plus traps were set along a course spanning more than 160 miles and took an entire day, with some dark on each end of it, to check and reset. And the number of furbearers he caught was amazing.

All of us who know Jim well know that come fall, when trapping season begins, he'll be hard to find, because every day he'll be in the river bottoms or on the mountain ridges, tending his lines. Depending on market and weather conditions, some years he mostly works the water, focusing on mink, muskrats, raccoons, otters, and other wetland furbearers. Other years he concentrates on bobcats, foxes, coyotes, and other animals on the higher ground. Most years he splits it up, doing some of each, because he loves all types of trapping so well he can't bring himself to forego any of it. That's my take on it, anyway.

Whatever species this modern mountain man goes after, he captures in good numbers. And having done this for decades, devoting hundreds of hours annually to his passion, he has gained a measure of experience few trappers will ever possess. He is probably not the best trapper in the world, but he's the best one I know, and I'd put him up against anyone in a head-to-head competition. Not that he'd have any of it, you understand; he traps for himself, for the joy of it, for the feeling that, as he told me once around one of those bourbon-sipping campfires, "because I feel like I'm helping to keep something alive."

This book you are about to read is one more example of Jim's striving to "keep something alive." No one is more qualified to write a book on trapping, and no one who ever did has done so with Jim's flair. Regardless of your skill level—beginner, veteran, or in between—you'll do well to follow the advice and examples set forth in the pages that follow. My prediction is not only will you become a better trapper, but also that this book is certain to become a favorite you'll return to again and again.

—Keith "Catfish" Sutton

Introduction

Why I Am a Trapper

They tell me I was born too late, that I should have been a mountain man, that I would have fit right in with the buckskin-clad loners who explored this land in their relentless quest for beaver pelts.

They tell me I'm an anachronism, that the day of my art has come and gone, that I'm a practitioner of an old-fashioned, outdated form of outdoor activity that has no place in the modern world.

They tell me, too, I'm a social misfit, that I'm a cruel and bloodthirsty perpetrator of an inhuman and inhumane activity, that my fellows and I should be thrown into jail like the criminals we are.

They tell me these things because I'm a trapper.

They're wrong.

First, I was not born too late, and I would not have made a good mountain man. Sure, I'd love to have seen the Ozarks as Friedrich Gerstäcker saw them in the 1830s and 1840s, with elk and bison in the cedar glades and a turkey behind every bush. And sometimes I daydream about the things Messrs. Lewis and Clark saw as they ascended the Missouri 200 years ago. John Colter, despite the balloon of legend that surrounds his name, doubtless saw a great many things I'd give ten years of my life to see.

But I'm too fond of flush toilets, air-conditioning, and Gore-Tex to wish I'd been born in the 1700s instead of the 1900s. Take away my insulated waders and my pickup truck and I'd wimp out on you in a hurry. I'm a Baby Boomer, born in the lap of solid middle-class comfort, and I'm not willing to pay the necessary price to step into H. G. Wells's time machine and turn it back a couple notches. Nope. No mountain man here.

Second, I'm no more anachronism than anaconda. It's true that trapping is an ancient profession. It's also true that trappers still use the same basic equipment their predecessors used 200 years ago. The opponents of trapping are quite correct when they claim there have been few significant changes in the basic leg-hold steel trap since its invention in medieval times as a device for catching poachers on the lands of European royalty. A Yankee blacksmith named Sewell Newhouse brought quality, consistency, and mass production to the trap-making business in the 1820s, but the basic steel trap is much the same today as it was when days were old and knights were bold.

Rather than use that as a condemnation, though, use it instead as a sign that trapping achieved state-of-the-art technology long before most other forms of outdoor recreation. The fact is, Mr. Newhouse merely refined an already efficient machine in the early 1800s. If he could come back and go with me on my trapline this winter, Newhouse would have no trouble recognizing the tools of the trade, because they've changed so little in appearance and function.

It's hard to improve on perfection, and so the leg-hold steel trap remains the most efficient—and, in many situations, the only—method of regulating populations of many species, or of removing specific problem animals from otherwise non-problem populations. The proverbial fox in the henhouse, for example.

In fact, far from having outlived its place, trapping may now be more important than ever in terms of protecting human interests from nuisance animals and regulating populations of some species to keep their numbers within the capacity of their habitat. Humans have intruded upon the natural world in a big way, and out-of-control wildlife populations can no longer be tolerated in many areas because they disrupt or inconvenience our human way of life. It's an arrogant attitude, but there you are.

But so far what we've been talking about are differences of opinion, and differences of opinion have never bothered me very much. That's why Baskin-Robbins has 31 flavors; that's why lawyers will always be with us.

What does bother me, though, is that last set of things "they" tell me: that I'm cruel, bloodthirsty, inhumane, and worse. I've been accosted at parties, at work, and other places by people who called me things they didn't know me well enough to call me.

It's not the name-calling that's troubling. What scratches going down is the fact that these people who berate me are mostly good, mostly decent, mostly intelligent people. They're not members of the lunatic fringe who blow up research labs and lurk around shopping malls throwing red paint on fur coats. Such felonious, wacko behavior is as far removed from them on the one hand as trapping is on the other.

But these, the misinformed, sincerely believe trapping is cruel and inhumane, and they're very concerned about the whole thing. Else they

The anti-trapping faction condemns the fact that there has been little change in the basic design of the foothold steel trap since it was invented. The reason isn't because of indifference, but because the original design was a pretty good one. Modern refinements have vastly improved the efficiency of the foothold trap, but the basic design remains much the same.

wouldn't accost me at parties and meetings. They wouldn't tell me they think I'm being cruel when I trap. This concern shows through in their voices, in the earnest look in their eyes. They want me and my kind to cease and desist. They want trapping outlawed forever.

Most folks apparently think we're just in it for the money, but trappers themselves know how ridiculous that notion is. Picking up aluminum cans on the side of the road pays better than trapping.

There are professional trappers among us, sure. There are also opportunists who join the ranks only when fur prices are high. But even when the market is good, not even the best of the best make enough from their traplines to support themselves and their families without working another job during the long off-season.

Getting paid for prime, well-handled furs is a nice perk of an enjoyable outdoor activity, but slinging fries at a fast-food joint is more profitable and less aggravating. In a two-week stretch of a recent trapping season, I spent $418.72 on supplies, equipment, and gasoline, and grossed—*grossed*, mind you—less than $1,100. That works out to something like four bucks an hour, twelve hours a day, seven days a week.

That's hardly CEO wages, but I've already told you I'm not out there for the money. I'm out there for . . . well, read on.

Please take note: I am not cruel and insensitive. I am not barbaric and bloodthirsty. Don't hang any halos on my head, because I assure you they don't belong there. However, the reasons they don't belong there have nothing to do with my being a trapper. My level of bloodlust is no higher—or lower—than that of the millions of my predecessors who have hunted, fished, and trapped for both recreation and livelihood down through the years of this country's birth and development. It's no higher or lower than yours.

I am a professional wildlife biologist. My professional training is in the management and control of wildlife populations—both upward and downward. Pro-trapping groups sometimes use this argument where it doesn't fit, but there are indeed many instances when trapping with snares, leg-hold traps, or killer-type traps is the only way to control certain problem animal populations.

The beaver is a prime example of a species that needs control, not only for its own good but also for the good of the humans who live in proximity to beavers. As proof that trapping is an effective control on this species, consider that the beaver was exterminated from most of North America because of over-trapping. Beavers were gone from large areas by the beginning of the Civil War, and the extermination was nearly complete by the beginning of the twentieth century. Isolated colonies hung on in remote regions of the Southeast, the Rockies, and Canada, but for the most part beavers existed only in tales told by grandfathers.

After a fifty-year hiatus, they came back. And they came with a vengeance. From a standing start of zero animals in most places, beaver populations climbed swiftly to epidemic proportions. The increase was unimpeded by predation, since natural predators such as bears, cougars, and wolves had also been exterminated and were never effective agents of beaver control anyway.

Since the frontier way of life was gone, and since beaver fur had become a cheap, barely marketable commodity, there was little trapping pressure. Beavers rapidly re-colonized their old home grounds, and beaver dams now span streams and block ditches from coast to coast and border to border.

Sorry if it offends anybody's sensibilities, but the only way to control beaver populations is trapping. You can dynamite beaver dams until you

From a low ebb of a mere few thousand survivors at the beginning of the twentieth century, beaver populations have rebounded nationwide and throughout most of Canada as well.

go deaf, and all you'll do is inconvenience the beavers. Go home after a hard day of blowing dams, and the beavers will repair the damage while you sleep.

Ditto with muskrats. They don't build dams, but they burrow like hyperthyroid gophers, and they give farmers, road builders, and pond owners fits. Again, there's no way to keep these prolific little fellows under control besides trapping them.

Otters in catfish ponds, skunks in chicken houses, raccoons in suburban attics—all these and more are instances where trapping is the only effective solution. However, as we've already mentioned, this old population control argument isn't always valid. In many instances, furbearer populations cause no problems and remain fairly stable and healthy whether they are trapped or not. Mink and bobcats are good examples. These are territorial, mostly solitary species, and the biology of their kind doesn't allow them to overpopulate except in the most unusual circumstances.

But note what I just said: populations of these animals would remain relatively stable whether they are trapped or not. Trapping is a consumptive use of these furbearer resources, no denying it. But when it's done legally, within guidelines established by wildlife resource agencies, trapping doesn't deplete populations of these animals. Natural reproduction replaces those individuals taken by trapping, just as it replaces those taken by predation and disease, and the circle of life rolls merrily on.

Most of us make every effort to trap as humanely as possible. Humane trapping is also efficient trapping, and it's just plain good business to do it this way. But in addition, most trappers realize the potential for pain and suffering, and we do everything we can to minimize it.

Most trappers use drowning sets or killer-type sets where possible, and we run our traps daily, as the law prescribes when these type sets can't be made. The result is not only less discomfort for the critter, but also a higher percentage of catches. The trapped animal doesn't have as much chance to fight the trap, injure itself, and possibly escape.

There are slob trappers out there, sure. But there are also slob drivers, and we don't all need to be banished from the highways because some fool wants to drive a hundred miles per hour and weave in and out of traffic. Neither should all trappers be penalized because some other fool sets an illegal trap with teeth on its jaws. Traffic regulations exist to control the dimwits, not the right-minded. Trapping regulations have a similar purpose.

I am no dimwit, or at least I don't think so, and therefore I try to follow not only the law but also my conscience. And that's why I have no

Modern trappers operate under close public scrutiny. We owe it not only to the animals we catch but also to ourselves and our fellow trappers to use the most humane trapping methods available.

problem, biologically, morally, or ethically, with being a trapper. I'm comfortable in the role of predator, and I don't feel ill at ease when I insert myself into the life cycles of various furbearers. On the contrary, I enjoy it; it makes me feel closer to the land. I'm a player, not a spectator.

I do my best to make each and every set as humane as possible, so the trapped animal will drown or be quickly killed, or will be securely held in a trap of the proper size, strength, and configuration to minimize injury and discomfort. Almost every other trapper of my acquaintance does these things, too, and I know hundreds of them.

I'm no Pollyanna. I realize that when the jaws of a steel trap snap on the foot of an animal, it hurts. I've caught my own hands and fingers in traps hundreds of times, so I know what I'm talking about here. I'd be lying if I said it was pleasant.

But natural death isn't too pleasant, either, if you happen to be, say, a muskrat. Substituting a quick drowning for being ripped to shreds by a great horned owl or eaten alive by a coyote doesn't seem like a bad deal. The muskrat might not take the deal if he had a choice, but it's the best I can offer. At least when I catch the muskrat in a trap, its fur gets used for warmth and beauty rather than as binder in a coyote's scat or a horned owl's pellet.

And in the process, I get to perform my chosen role of predator, player, and participant in the web of life.

Part I

PREPARING YOUR TRAPLINE

1

What to Expect From Your Trapline

Americans are accustomed to instant gratification. We're addicted to the quick fix. Not only do we want to have our cake and eat it, too, but also we want it right now.

This is never more apparent than in outdoor-type TV programs, videos, and DVDs, whether they're about fishing, hunting, or trapping. Watch a TV fishing show, and the host catches a bass on every cast. On a hunting show, a turkey gobbler is heard, approached, called to, shot, and displayed before the camera, all in five minutes. Viewers want action, and that's what we get. All the dead time of the fishing trip or the turkey hunt is edited out. What's left is a few minutes of action-packed excitement.

Magazine articles and books also play to the quick-fix attitude. Do a, b, and c, and you'll get d. The trouble is, a magazine piece has about 2,000 words, and takes 15 minutes to read. A book like this one takes a little longer, but still the process is fairly quick. And when you get to the end, presto! Problem solved. Critter reduced to possession.

Experienced outdoor types know things don't happen that way in real life. Bass don't jump on lures as frequently as they appear to do on the TV screen. Real-time turkey hunts don't unfold as quickly as they do on The Outdoor Channel. Also, a, b, and c in a magazine piece or book don't always add up to d in the real world. Even when they do, the addition process takes a lot longer than reading about it.

But visual and written images are powerful things. After we've watched a few outdoor shows or videos, after we've read a few how-to magazine articles packed with condensed, rapid-fire instruction and action, we start getting impatient when things don't happen so fast. We start pushing. We expect too much. And we make mistakes because we're in such an all-fired hurry to succeed.

The volume of how-to information available to today's trapper is staggering—books, videos, DVDs, personal instruction, magazine articles. But when all is said and done, the best way to become an efficient trapper is to get out there and get your hands dirty.

Trapping videos and DVDs suffer from the same built-in problem. People watch them for two reasons: first, to learn more effective (or at least different) techniques for catching furbearers; second, for entertainment. And the way to make a trapping video both educational and entertaining is to film a lot of catches. Checking empty trap after empty trap may be realistic, but it doesn't have much instructional value. Nor will it hold a viewer's attention very long.

But, again, all that artificially condensed action creates a false impression. It makes it look like the trapper in the video catches more animals— or at least has a higher catch ratio—than is actually the case. But just as there are a lot of no-action minutes and hours that don't get filmed in the making of a TV fishing show, there are plenty of empty traps and unvisited sets that don't make it onto a trapping video either. When a trapper and his cameraman are shooting footage for a video, they look at many sets that don't contain any furbearers for every one that does. Guess which ones get filmed?

In the late 1980s, after I produced the first of four mink trapping videos, it didn't take long for trappers to start asking me questions that indicated they were looking for a quick fix to mink trapping success. The questions varied widely, but the basic theme was the same: "What's your secret?" In other words, "How can I catch a pile of mink fast, without working too hard at it?"

The answer is straightforward, simple, honest . . . and entirely unsatisfactory to a quick-fix addict: "You can't." Or at least I can't. The only way I've found to catch mink in decent numbers—or any other furbearer, for that matter—is to get out there early, stay out there late, and work very hard in between. That's an oversimplification, of course, but it contains a basic truth. You're not going to get more out of your trapline than you're willing to put into it.

THEORY VS. OJT

Technique is important, sure. That's the first stumbling block in the path of the quick-fix approach to efficient, productive trapping. In order to consistently catch any species of furbearer, the trapper must have not

Catches like this, whether it's mink or any other furbearer, don't come to those who don't work at it.

only a working knowledge of that animal's habits, but also a solid grasp of proper trapping methods. If you don't have a firm grip on these two things, it won't matter how many hours you spend on the trapline. You could trap 24-7 and still not catch much.

The thing is, this knowledge isn't sold in bottles, like vitamin pills or Gatorade. Sure, there's a lot more information out there on furbearer life history and on trapping technique than when we graybeards were growing up in the 1940s, 1950s, and 1960s, and for the most part it's pretty good information. The intelligence is available, all right. But here's something sad but true: knowing something because you've read it or watched it and knowing something because you've lived it are vastly different things.

"In some ways, all this information is a disadvantage to beginning and intermediate hunters, because they can watch videos and read books and magazines and come away thinking they know a lot," a friend of mine said one time. "But the real teacher is walking around out there right now, while we're sitting here talking about him. You think you can learn it from your easy chair, but all you can really learn is the theory. You think you understand that, but that penetrates only so far until you get out there and get your nose rubbed in it a few hundred times."

My buddy was talking about turkeys instead of furbearers, but the principle is the same, be it longbeards or lynx, mallards or mink. Hearing the words and watching the techniques on a TV screen are a good start, but you don't really learn the lessons until you've put in some on-the-job training, and until you've enrolled in the school of hard knocks. Which, by the way, offers no degree, because the learning process never stops.

EVALUATE THE POTENTIAL OF YOUR TERRITORY
No matter how much expertise you develop as a trapper, though, you can't conjure up more critters than your trapline has available. Knowledge, expertise, and elegant technique can't make up for a shortage of targets. Drop the best beaver trapper in the world in the middle of the Mojave Desert, and he won't need many beaver stretchers.

Competition from other trappers can also limit your catch. If there were one hundred raccoons on a stretch of river and other trappers take half of them before you come along, your catch won't be as high as it would have been if you had the river all to yourself.

If your area had a high raccoon population last year but distemper got into them over the spring and summer, you're not going to have as many raccoons to work with this year. If you had a severe spring and summer drought, expect your local muskrat population to be down. Things like that influence your catch.

Of course, there's not much a trapper can do about furbearer population densities or competition from other trappers. You can shift from one species to another in response to population swings and fur prices, but if target furbearers are scarce in your part of the world, you won't catch as many as the guy who's trapping where those species are abundant. If you have competition from other trappers (and who doesn't?), there's not much you can do but accept that you'll be splitting the potential of your line with those other trappers.

FIGHTING THE ELEMENTS

Weather, too, enters into any projection of a trapline's potential. Bad weather and inclement conditions must be figured into the equation when you're trying to figure out how much fur you can take from a given area. How many days of bad weather do you think you'll have? Nobody knows the answer, of course, but you can guess at it, based on normal fall and winter weather patterns.

TIME AND ATTITUDE

How many days, weeks, or months will you trap? How many hours a day will you spend at it? Any trapper with average intelligence and enough coordination to set a steel trap can climb the learning curve and become fairly good at catching critters—this isn't quantum physics, after all—but we can't control things like distemper, drought, and weather conditions.

Nor can we always control the time factor. We might gain a little trapline time by cutting something else on the schedule, but job, family obligations, rest requirements, and the fact there are only 24 hours in each day make it inevitable that at some point, trapline time is limited. Nobody can trap around the clock, not even professional long-liners.

There are few of those, anyway. Most modern-day trappers are, by necessity or choice, part-time, shortline trappers. Most trappers run a dozen to three dozen sets before or after school or work, usually for no longer than two or three weeks. And this one simple factor affects the potential of their traplines more than any other. No matter how well he's mastered the art and science of trapping, a part-timer running twenty-five sets for two weeks isn't going to catch as much fur as a less skilled trapper who's running ten times as much steel for the entire length of the trapping season. Catching a larger pile of fur doesn't mean the full-time trapper is better. It just means he has more chances.

A "good season's catch" isn't measured exclusively by body count. Instead, it's relative and must be measured against the size of a trapline, the length of time spent trapping, the relative scarcity of abundance of furbearers, and other factors. Who's the best? All of us are, as long as we give it our best shot.

KEEPING IT IN PERSPECTIVE

Every trapper owes it to himself and to the furbearers he pursues to become as skilled and knowledgeable as possible. This is not difficult; as we've already mentioned, this ain't quantum physics. The amount of time available for trapping and the willingness to use that time to maximum advantage are also controllable, or at least partly so. But all the rest of it is out of our hands. The best we can do is factor it into the evaluation process and judge our performance in terms of how well we're doing with relative to what we have to work with.

What it all boils down to is that trapline success can't be measured by body count alone. Who's the best trapper? You are, as long as you do the best you can, under the conditions imposed by your trapline.

2

Appropriate Traps
for Various Furbearers

Except for learning how to actually catch things, the most confusing part of trapping for the newcomer is probably figuring out what traps to use for each animal. A quick glance through any trapping magazine or supply catalog reveals a bewildering array of trap brands, sizes, and styles. Within the sizes and styles, there are further variations in the design of jaws, pans, swivels, chains, and practically every other part of the trap.

A good part of this diversity is understandable, especially the differences in trap sizes, because furbearers come in different sizes and shapes. It doesn't take a modern-day Jim Bridger to know weasel traps should be a little smaller than coyote traps.

But beyond that, the array of trap sizes and styles still bewilders the beginner, and sometimes the veteran as well. Many of the trap styles that have come and gone over the years have been complicated or gimmicky, designed more to catch trappers than to catch fur. A few have stood the test of time, however. There's more discussion about trap sizes and styles in the chapters dealing with trapping the various species, but here's a brief rundown of the most popular and most effective traps available today:

LONGSPRING FOOTHOLD TRAPS
Excepting the deadfall, the longspring trap is the oldest design. It was used in medieval Europe to catch human poachers on royal estates, and it's still used today, in various sizes, for every North American furbearer. Longspring traps have single or double springs, but most traps in the larger sizes are doubles.

Longspring traps are easier to bed solidly when making sets, because of the larger trap area in contact with the ground. They are also heavier, size for size, than other styles, an advantage for drowning sets but a disadvantage on a walking or small-boat trapline.

The basic design of the foothold trap has changed little over the years, but there have still been a lot of modifications to make certain traps more suitable for the various sizes and types of furbearers.

Number 0 single longspring traps have a jaw spread of approximately 3½ inches and are suitable only for the smallest furbearers—weasel, maybe muskrat, and in some tight places they can be effectively used for mink.

Number 1 single longspring traps have a jaw spread of about 4 inches and are used mostly for muskrat, weasel, opossum, and skunk. Some mink, marten, and raccoon trappers use them, too.

Number 11 longsprings also have a jaw spread of about 4 inches, but have two springs instead of one. These small but strong traps can hold large, powerful animals like beaver and otter if the trap gets a secure grip on the animal's foot, but the small jaw spread makes it a poor choice for large animals, except for live capture of otter. The number 11 is the favorite of many mink and coon trappers and is also sometimes used for fox, marten, and fisher.

Number 1½ longsprings are single spring traps with a 4¾-inch jaw spread. Once one of the most popular traps, the 1½ longspring has largely been replaced by the 1½ coilspring. The 1½ longspring is used mostly for muskrats, but it's also suitable for mink, opossum, skunk, nutria, marten, and fisher, and at secure drowning sets for raccoon.

The number 2 longspring is a 1½ longspring with a second spring added. It is stronger, naturally, and can be used for the same furbearers as the 1½, plus fox, coyote, badger, and bobcat.

Number 3 and 4 longsprings are larger, double-spring traps with jaw spreads of approximately 5½ and 6 inches, respectively. Until the introduction of the coilspring style, the number 3 longspring was a favorite of many coyote trappers and is still the favorite of some. Both 3 and 4 longsprings are also suitable for beaver, otter, and bobcat.

The number 5 longspring, with its 7½-inch jaw spread, is the largest foothold trap allowed in most states and provinces. It is an excellent beaver trap and is effective for otter as well.

COILSPRING FOOTHOLD TRAPS

A relatively new design in foothold traps, coilsprings were introduced in the middle part of the twentieth century. Because they are more compact and slightly lighter than longsprings, coilsprings quickly gained a following. For years, though, coilsprings were restricted to the smaller trap sizes, and beaver/otter/wolf-size coilsprings didn't become widely available or popular until the late 1980s and early 1990s. Today, it would be a hard call to say whether there are more coilsprings or longsprings in use.

Coilsprings are generally faster than longsprings, and their more compact construction makes them easier to conceal and use in tight places. They are also simple and easy to assemble and disassemble, which facilitates field repair and adjustment.

Coilsprings are available in 1, 1½, 1¾, 2, 3, 4, 650, and 750. The jaw spreads of the smaller sizes are roughly equal to the corresponding longspring sizes, and they're used for the same animals. The 650 has a jaw spread of 6½ inches, and the 750 a spread of 7½ inches. These large traps are used for coyote, wolf, beaver, and otter.

GUARD-TYPE FOOTHOLD TRAPS

Available in both longspring and coilspring models, guard-type traps have a spring-powered, U-shaped lever that comes up over the jaws of the trap after it springs, usually with a delayed-action feature triggered when the trapped animal pulls the chain tight. The lever pins the trapped animal's leg against the trap jaws and frame and prevents it from either chewing off or twisting off its foot to escape. Primarily designed for shallow-water muskrat trapping, guard traps are also effective in preventing chew-outs from raccoons.

These traps are only made in smaller sizes, number 1 and sometimes 1½. They are more expensive, harder to conceal, more complicated to adjust and repair, and are not widely used. However, a few guard traps are a useful addition to most water traplines.

BODY-GRIPPER TRAPS

Although there were previous attempts, it wasn't until the 1950s that a Canadian trapper named Frank Conibear perfected and patented the basic design that is the standard for body-gripping traps today—a square-jawed trap with a stiff wire trigger. When the target animal passes through the trap jaws and hits the trigger wires, the trap snaps on the animal's head, neck, or body. Both single- and double-spring models are available in the smaller sizes, and the larger sizes are almost always double springs.

Widely copied and much modified by other manufacturers, the original Conibear design is still evident in most body-grippers, and the word "Conibear" is used as a generic term to describe body-gripper traps of all brands. Round-jawed body-grippers are also manufactured, but the most popular design is the square-jawed model.

Size designation numbers vary from manufacturer to manufacturer, but the five most common jaw spread sizes are 4½-inch, 6-inch, 7-inch, 8-inch, and 10-inch.

The 4½-inch body-gripper comes in both single-spring and double-spring models (it's the only body-gripper currently manufactured in single-spring) and is used mostly for mink, muskrat, and marten trapping. This size is also effective on opossum and skunk and on smaller non-furbearing mammals like squirrels and rabbits.

The 6-inch size is used mostly for raccoon but also for marten, fisher, opossum, skunk, and underwater sets for muskrat and mink. The 7-inch body-gripper is good for otter, fisher, raccoon, bobcat, and in tight-fitting sets for beaver, although its jaw spread is generally a little too small for most beaver trapping situations. The 8-inch size is the choice of many otter trappers and is also good for raccoon, bobcat and beaver. The 10-inch size is primarily a beaver trap, but is also good for otter.

SNARES

Snares were being used to capture animals even before deadfalls and longspring foothold traps. The earliest snares were natural lengths of vine or braided cord made of sinew, plant fibers, hair, and other natural materials. Modern trappers use braided steel cable, varying in diameter from ⅛-inch down to ³⁄₆₄-inch, to capture everything from timber wolves to weasels.

CAGE TRAPS

The earliest cage traps were elongated wooden boxes. The animal bumped and dislodged a notched trigger while attempting to reach the bait, causing a sliding door to fall into place behind the animal. Farm boys nationwide used these "rabbit gums" to put meat on the table, and they caught an occasional possum, skunk, and raccoon as well. These traps are still being made by hand and effectively used, but by a much smaller number of people. Modern cage traps operate on the same gen-

Modern cage traps are usually made of wire mesh or PVC plastic, but the basic design is much the same today is it was 75 years ago: the animal attempts to get a bait placed in the rear, triggering the trap and getting caught in the process.

eral principle, but the traps are made of wire and reinforcement rod and the door falls when the animal steps on a foot treadle.

The other commonly used cage trap is the colony trap, used primarily for catching muskrats in underwater runs and den entrances. It operates on the trapdoor principle; with the swimming muskrat entering the trap by pushing one of the two slanting doors open. The door falls closed behind the 'rat and prevents it from leaving the trap. Multiple catches are common with colony traps, and mink are sometimes captured as well.

Cage traps in general are large, bulky, expensive, and harder to hide than standard traps and snares. This makes them unsuitable for most trapline situations. However, they are extensively used in urban or suburban nuisance animal control work, or anywhere else where free-roaming domestic animals are likely. Cage traps are not very effective for the more wary furbearers such as foxes, coyotes, and otters.

K.I.S.S.

This isn't a reference to the old heavy metal band, but rather to a basic principle of sound trapping. You're going to see it again and again in these pages. It stands for "Keep it simple, stupid," and remembering this one thing will save a trapper time, grief, and money. Simple beats complicated almost every time. Our tendency as trappers—at least my tendency as a trapper—is to make things too complicated. When I'm on the trapline, I have to remind myself several times daily of the K.I.S.S. rule.

One of the best ways to K.I.S.S. is by standardizing trap sizes and styles. No trapline, even when you're exclusively targeting a single species, can be effectively covered with only one size and style of trap, but neither is there a need to have a dozen types of traps when three will suffice. Standardization of equipment streamlines things, which saves time, which leads to efficiency, which translates into a more favorable bottom line. Think about your trapping conditions, narrow down your trap styles to the minimum required to get the job done, and you'll reduce your trapline headaches. It's as simple as that.

TRAP MODIFICATION, ADJUSTMENT, AND TREATMENT

A few trap manufacturers have made the advertising claim that their traps were ready to go to the trapline "right out of the box." Don't believe it. Every brand, size, or style of factory trap can be improved by a little knowledgeable tinkering. Even if there were a perfect trap, it still wouldn't be ready right out of the box because it would still have factory grease on it, and it wouldn't be protected from rusting.

Regardless of the claims of the manufacturer, no trap is ready to go right out of the box.

Granted, this is the way many trappers operate—using traps right out of the box. Even some veterans of many years on the line don't bother to modify, adjust, or even clean the oil and metal shavings off their traps. When the season closes, they put their traps up still caked with mud and dirt, and that's the way they start setting them when the next season comes.

These trappers catch fur. Some catch a lot of fur. But when I see a trapper treating his equipment so carelessly, I always wonder how much more this guy would catch if he'd fine-tune and treat his traps, and how much money he'd save on equipment if he took a few steps to protect his traps from rust before using them. The probable answer to both questions is "quite a bit."

Modern manufacturing processes produce remarkably uniform and consistent products, and this is as true with traps as with television sets. But a TV doesn't just start working perfectly when you take it out of the box and plug it in. It must first run through its internal programming functions, and then you must hook it up to a receiving instrument of some sort—cable company, satellite company, metal antenna. Only then will the set work properly. That doesn't mean the TV is faulty. It just has to be tweaked, that's all. The same thing is true of factory traps. They'll work straight out of the box, but they'll work much better if they're adjusted and treated.

Pre-Adjustment Cleaning

The logical order is to make the physical changes and mechanical adjustments to your traps before boiling, dyeing, dipping, or waxing them, since one of the objectives of treating traps is ridding them of objectionable odors. However, since traps fresh out of the box are often heavily coated with a sooty film of grease, fine metal shavings, and other stuff, they can be messy to work with. If you want to really ruin a pair of blue jeans and a t-shirt, just wear them for an afternoon of working on

Boiling traps in soapy or caustic water to remove contaminants like blood, factory oil, and grease is the logical first step of trap preparation.

a few dozen brand-new traps. On the other hand, this stuff won't hurt you. If you don't mind it, fine, but if you'd rather get your traps a little cleaner before working on them, there are several ways to go about it.

Burying the traps in a pile of wet leaves is an easy way to get rid of most of this factory residue, if time isn't a factor. Just cover the traps well and keep the leaves wet for a week or two. The tannin in the leaves forms a weak acid that eats away the greasy coating. It will also usually start the rusting process, so don't leave the traps in the wet leaves too long.

Alternatively, you can take greasy new traps to the local self-serve car wash, lay over the grate, and give them a thorough soapy washing. This is the fastest method. Or, you can degrease factory-fresh traps by running them through a cycle in the dishwasher. Be sure the chains aren't hanging down into the moving parts. Depending on trap size, an average dishwasher can hold three traps, or three dozen. This method works well and won't harm the dishwasher, but it might create problems on the domestic front. Use discretion if you try this method; mothers, wives, and girlfriends sometimes don't think this is an appropriate use of a kitchen appliance.

Leghold Trap Adjustment and Modification

First, set and spring each trap to make sure it works. Next, give the trap a close visual inspection. Are the jaws level with each other when the trap is sprung? If not, lay a flat piece of hardwood across the jaws and tap it with a hammer to drive the jaws down until they're even.

Do the ends of the jaws protrude far enough through the ends of the bottom plate so that they won't pop out during the struggles of a trapped animal? If not, follow the procedure above to drive the jaws a little lower and force the ends farther through the bottom plate.

Next, use a sturdy pair of pliers or crimpers to squeeze the eye of the trap dog tighter, where it's attached to the dog arm. Don't close the eye down so far that the dog binds and won't work smoothly, but do take any extra play out of the circle. This adjustment makes it impossible for the dog to shift in relation to the dog arm and removes the possibility of "pan creep."

Next, file the dog and pan notch square, as shown in the illustration. Trap parts are stamped rather than cut, and the stamping process results in rounded or roughed-up edges. The traps spring fine, but there's often a lot of pan creep before they do. Filing the dog and notch square produces a smooth, precise fit between these parts, resulting in a clean, crisp firing action.

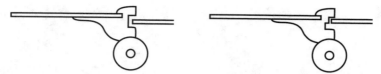

Trap dogs and pan notches should be filed square to eliminate pan creep when a furbearer steps in the trap. Some trappers file an extra notch, known as a "night latch," (right) but this is an unnecessary refinement.

Some trappers file a second, shorter notch into the pan notch, called a "night latch." The idea is to create a stair-step configuration inside the notch so the trapper can set the trap, and then, without having to look at it, slowly pull the pan down with his thumb until he hears the dog snap into the second notch. When this happens, the trap produces an audible click, and the trap is now on a hair trigger—in other words, it will fire with very little additional pan travel.

The night latch is a good idea, but it's too complicated. You can accomplish the same thing by filing the end of the pan notch down until there's only a very short lip to hold the dog in place when the trap is set. A trap thus adjusted is automatically hair-triggered, and the step of pulling the pan down into the night latch is eliminated—as is the need to file the night latch into the notch in the first place. Keep it simple, remember? Strictly speaking, neither the night latch nor the short notch is necessary, but both these modifications add a degree of uniformity to the way your traps will fire, and that's never a bad thing.

The final step in pan adjustment is to make sure the pan sits level. Set the trap again. The pan should be level when the trap is level, and the pan height should be about the same height as the upper surfaces of the trap jaws. A little lower is okay, a little higher is not okay. If the pan angle is too high, bend the trap's dog arm toward the jaws. If the pan is too low, bend the dog arm away from the jaws. Be conservative with the bending; a little movement in the dog arm alters the pan height considerably.

Few traps come from the factory with adequate chains. The proper modification depends on the intended use of the trap and on the trapper's individual style and preferences, but here's the way I do it: First, I cut the chain at the second link from the trap (we're assuming double-link chain here, the most common kind). Then I use two bent rivets and a double box swivel to attach the one link of chain remaining on the trap to two more links of chain. The last step is to attach a universal swivel to the other end of the two links, again using a bent rivet. This produces about eight inches of trap chain with an in-line swivel. It's efficient and

Adding an in-line swivel to the trap chain is a worthwhile investment, as long as the added swivel is close to the trap. One or two links of chain between trap and swivel is just about right.

versatile and works equally well on land and water, on stakes, slide wires, or extension chain with drags or grapples.

There are many more possible leghold trap modifications, some of them pretty complicated. Laminating the jaws by welding or bolting an additional piece of metal to the jaws is one popular modification, especially for raccoon and coyote trappers. The purpose is to increase the amount of jaw surface that contacts the animal's foot, thus increasing holding power and reducing pull-outs. Laminating jaws is time-consuming, though, and the increased surface area of the jaws means the jaws have to travel through more dirt or water, slowing the action. It also increases the chance that the trap will become clogged with debris or dirt and fail to close properly.

Some experienced and accomplished trappers move the chain attachment to the bottom of the trap, using either a short length of chain around the base plate or a rivet through a hole bored through the base plate. Again, the objective is to reduce losses. But this method results in a trap that is harder to bed in firm or rocky ground, because the bottom of the trap has trap chain attached and is no longer smooth and level.

Both of the above modifications increase the holding power of a trap, but in my opinion there's a better, simpler way to modify your coil-springs: just use stronger springs. Some trappers add an extra set of coilsprings (four-coiling kits are commercially available) but the easiest method, and the one I prefer, is simply replacing the factory springs with springs designed for a larger trap. I install number 3 coilsprings on my 1¾s, and put the 1¾ springs on my 1½s. The result is a fast, powerful trap that doesn't weigh any more and doesn't have an uneven bottom surface, but holds as well as any trap of its size.

Body-Gripper Adjustment and Modification

As with footholds, make sure each trap operates properly. Some body-grippers fresh from the factory won't stay set. The most common reason is that the notches in the trap dog aren't deep enough to hold the opposite trap jaw securely. Fortunately, this defect is easy to fix by using a rat-tail file to make the notch a little deeper.

Another occasional defect shows up in the rivets or bolts that hold the trap jaws together at the hinge. Again, this is easy to correct. Simply drill the old rivet out and replace it with a carriage bolt and nut of the proper dimension, with the head of the bolt on the inside of the jaws.

Adding a swivel to the chain of larger body-grippers (160 to 330) is a good investment. It's not as important with 110-sized traps, but if you don't add a swivel to the chain of your larger body-grippers, it's going to cost you. Body-gripper traps are designed to kill the target animal, but it doesn't always happen quickly, and sometimes not at all. When a catch is still alive in the trap, it will twist and fight. Body-grippers come from the factory with the chain attached directly to the trap spring, and this often results in a tightly twisted chain with no swiveling action.

To add a swivel, remove all but one link of chain from the trap and insert a box swivel into the chain as described in the leghold section above. Then replace the remainder of the chain (short or long, as you wish), add a universal swivel on the end opposite the trap, and you've vastly improved the holding power of any body-gripper during non-lethal captures.

One final modification to 110-size body-grippers used for mink trapping is extremely important: looping the triggers. It's also wise when using 280 and 330 body-grippers for otter. These two animals sometimes go through standard body-grippers without getting caught, or else they get so far through they're caught by the hips or back legs. The result is a live animal in the trap, which can lead to fur and trap theft, fur damage,

Using a short piece of fine wire or mono-filament fishing line to loop the triggers of small body-grippers makes them much more efficient and ensures a head and neck catch on mink, muskrats, and other small animals.

the escape of the captured animal, or worse, the escape of the captured animal still wearing the trap.

Looping a body-gripper's trigger is easy. Simply string a length of wire or monofilament fishing line between the two wires of the trigger. My preference is small-diameter craft wire, available at hobby and craft shops. It's sturdy and can be wrapped around the trigger wires, but fishing line must be tied on.

Whatever you use, first roughen the ends of the wire triggers, so the wire or line won't slip off. Rough sandpaper or a coarse file is good for this, or you can score the wires with a pair of cutting pliers. Some trappers flatten the ends of the wires and drill a tiny hole through the flattened portion, but this is tedious and too complicated, and the end result is no better. Remember the K.I.S.S. rule.

Post-Adjustment Trap Treatment

After your traps are modified and adjusted, it's time for the last steps to make them the best they can possibly be: cleaning, coloring, and waxing.

Cleaning

This step removes the factory grease from new traps and also removes dirt, blood, and other odors from both new and old traps. It's a good idea for footholds and body-grippers alike, and there are several ways to do it.

Two quick ways to get the job done have already been discussed—taking the traps to a self-serve car wash or running them through a cycle in the dishwasher. A better alternative, however, is to boil your traps in a large container, such as a clean, cut-in-half 55-gallon or 30-gallon metal drum, using a propane fish cooker. Propane is faster, safer, and allows better heat control than wood.

Obviously, this is an outside job, and should be done by an adult or with adult supervision. Select an open area, away from dry weeds or other flammables. Put the traps in the barrel, cover with clean water, and bring to a boil. Plain water can be used, but you'll get a cleaner end product if you use dishwashing soap or some other form of cleanser in

All trap treatment procedures requiring heating water or wax should be done outside. Caution should be observed throughout the process, and young trappers should always have adult supervision.

the water. Heavily rusted traps can be greatly improved by using caustic soda, but if you go this route, be sure to add the chemical to the water while the water is cold, and avoid getting any water in your eyes or mouth or on your hands.

Let the traps boil vigorously for 30 minutes or more, then turn off the heat and let the traps stand in the water for another 10 minutes. A film of oil and other contaminants will appear on the surface. Don't lift the traps out of the water through this film, or they'll be re-contaminated. Instead, fill the barrel to overflowing, washing the film over the sides and out of the barrel. Then remove the traps by hooking them with a garden rake or similar tool, lay them on a large piece of cardboard or plywood, and rinse them thoroughly.

If time allows, let the clean traps rust lightly before coloring them. This makes for a better coloring job, regardless of which of the following methods is used. However, don't let the traps rust too much or you'll need to repeat the boiling/cleaning process.

Dyeing

Dyeing traps works for both footholds and body-grippers. There are many methods, but the most effective is by boiling the traps again in water containing walnut hulls, sumac berries, maple leaves, or a commercial product known variously as logwood extract, logwood crystals, or logwood dye. Put the traps and the coloring agent in a barrel, cover with clean water, and boil vigorously for 30 minutes to an hour. Remove the traps when they're well colored, hang them to dry, and put another batch of traps in, adding more coloring agent as necessary. Traps can also be dyed in cold water, but it usually takes two or three weeks.

Both hot and cold dyeing methods work, but they're messy and slow, and trappers who do it this way are ignoring the K.I.S.S. rule. There's a better way.

Cold Dipping

The cold dipping method of trap coloring has largely taken the place of dyeing and involves using a black, brown, or white product to coat traps. The coating both colors the traps and protects them from rust.

Most cold-dip products are petroleum-based and require dilution with gasoline, lantern fuel, or mineral spirits, so extreme caution is necessary. Keep the solution away from flames or sparks, and make sure you're in an open, well-ventilated area. At least one company makes a water-based cold dip in both brown and black, and while it's safer to use, it's considerably more expensive.

Both petroleum-based and water-based products are applied in the same manner: First, dilute the dip according to the manufacturer's instructions, using a resealable container large enough to accommodate your largest trap. A five-gallon plastic bucket with a lid and a bail handle is ideal. Using a hook, bent wire or string, lower your traps either singly or in small bunches into the dip. Remove them immediately, shake them over the container and allow the excess liquid to drip off, then either hang the traps or lay them on a board or cardboard and allow them to dry.

Traps colored with water-based dip usually dry overnight, but petroleum-based dip takes longer—sometimes a week or more. Also, it takes that long for the petroleum and gasoline odor to dissipate. If you want petroleum-dipped traps to dry faster, add about 25 percent more diluting agent to the dip than the manufacturer advises when mixing it. This isn't a bad idea anyway, since the manufacturers usually recommend a dilution ratio that produces a fairly thick coating and, coincidentally, uses more of their product.

Some dips produce a slick, hard finish on traps, and for this reason many trappers don't dip their body-grippers, claiming the coating makes the trap dog and jaw too slippery and makes the traps fire too easily. I've rarely experienced this problem. When it does occasionally occur, it's easily corrected with a touch of sandpaper to the contact surfaces of the dog and jaw.

Painting

Painting is a quick-fix method, but it works pretty well on both footholds and body-grippers. Lay the clean traps as close together as possible on a clean, flat surface (the plywood or cardboard used in the cleaning process will work fine). Set all the footholds. Using spray cans of flat black, flat brown, olive drab, tan, or a combination of these colors, paint the traps thoroughly. Switch colors every few swipes to produce a camouflage effect if desired.

When painting body-gripper traps, turn them over and paint both sides. It's not necessary to paint the bottom side of foothold traps. Allow the traps to dry thoroughly before hanging them or storing them.

Waxing

It's not recommended for body-gripper traps, but waxing is the final touch for making footholds as efficient as they can possibly be, regardless of whether they'll be used in water or on land. It makes them faster and protects them from rusting better than any other method.

An old trapper's tale says that using pure paraffin for waxing traps produces a brittle coating that flakes off in cold weather. It's not true. Plain paraffin canning wax, available at grocery stores, works wonderfully. It's also usually less expensive than trap wax available from trapper supply dealers—which is made mostly of paraffin anyway.

Like boiling and cold dipping with petroleum-based dips, waxing traps is potentially dangerous and should only be done in a well-ventilated area, away from flammable substances, with adult supervision. Use gloves and protective eyewear at all times.

Precise heat control is much more important for waxing than when boiling or dyeing, so wood fires are unwise. Also, before starting to heat the wax, have a flat piece of board or sheet metal handy that is large enough to completely cover the waxing pot with at least a six-inch margin, in case the wax flashes and catches fire.

Using a flat-topped metal container large enough to accommodate your largest trap, melt the wax over a camp stove or propane fish cooker. Be sure the top of the container is smooth and flat so the cover will fit snugly over it in case of a wax fire. A deep, narrow pot is better for waxing than a wide, shallow one, because the same amount of melted wax will be deeper in a narrower pot. When the melted wax barely begins to smoke, use a stiff piece of hooked wire or other tool to slowly lower clean, dry traps into the container. Leave the traps in the wax until they're the same temperature as the wax, or they'll take on too much wax and it will flake off. A couple of minutes is usually long enough. Then hook the traps out and hold them over the pot to let the excess wax drip off. Hang the traps on a drying rack until they cool to air temperature.

When a trap is waxed properly, it will look wet when it cools. If the coat of wax is too thick, the trap will have a milky or cloudy coating. Wax any such traps again, leaving them in the hot wax for a longer period.

If the wax gets too hot, it may flash and start burning on the surface, causing flames to leap out of the pot. This is startling, but there's no need for panic. Quickly turn off the heat source. Wearing gloves and eye protection, carefully lay the edge of your cover board or sheet metal on the near edge of the pot, then slide it slowly and smoothly across the top until the pot is covered. Let the wax cool for 10 minutes or so, then remove the cover, take out the traps, relight the fire, and continue.

Using a double boiler system is a safer way of waxing traps, since the water bath of the double boiler won't allow the wax to get hotter than 212 degrees. It's safer, maybe, but the double boiler method doesn't allow either the wax or the trap to get hot enough to produce that thin, wet-looking coat of wax that works best. If you're nervous about the

Leave traps in the wax until they reach the same temperature as the wax. A minute is usually long enough for small traps, two minutes for larger ones. Hot traps take on a very thin coat of wax, which is the desired result.

possibility of a wax fire, use the double boiler method, but your wax job will be inferior.

Some trappers use commercial liquid floor wax. The clean traps are dipped in the floor-waxing product and hung to dry. I tried this once, but the wax coating was too thick for my preference, and the jaws and other moving parts had to be broken free when the traps were set for the first time. Also, I could still smell the floor wax on my traps, even several months after treatment. For my money, this isn't a satisfactory method.

Pick and Choose Your Methods
No one trap needs all the modifications and treatments we've discussed here, of course. Some traps require far less tweaking than others when they come out of the box, even when you're looking at traps of the same brand, packed in the box beside each other. There's no sense in doing

something to a trap when the trap doesn't need it. Remember our old friend Mr. K.I.S.S.

Likewise, in many cases it's okay to eliminate some of the post-adjustment treatments. For example, as we've already discussed, waxing body-grippers is inadvisable because it makes them too sensitive and touchy. It's also unnecessary to color traps that will be used in covered dirt sets, since the animal can't see the trap anyway. Eliminate that step, and proceed directly from cleaning to waxing.

The most important thing about trap adjustment and treatment is to recognize that a certain amount of it is desirable if you plan to run an efficient trapline. Get it done, and reap the benefits.

3

Trap Fastening and Swiveling Techniques

The best trap in the world isn't worth the dirt it's covered with unless it is effectively fastened. It does no good to catch an animal if the animal gets out of the trap or carries the trap away so it can't be recovered.

That seems like a no-brainer, but improper trap fastening techniques are responsible for more furbearer losses, including pull-outs, chew-offs, wring-offs, and lost traps, than anything else. More than improper trapping technique, more than using the wrong size traps, more even than trapline theft. This is completely unnecessary. There's always an effective, sure way to fasten a trap, no matter what kind of soil, water, or weather conditions are present. Maybe that's the root of the problem: there are so many choices, it's easy to make the wrong one.

STAKING TRAPS

By far the most common method, staking is just what it sounds like—fastening the trap to a wooden or metal stake, then driving the stake into the ground at the set location. It sounds simple, but even here there are many choices.

In good dirt—basically, the sort of stuff you like to have in a garden plot—a stake made of hardwood or metal (usually ½-inch or ⅜-inch concrete reinforcement rod, called "rebar" by most trappers) is sufficient, provided it's long enough to hold the largest animal that might be caught in the trap. For fox, 15-inch stakes are usually sufficient; for larger, more powerful animals like coyotes, 30- to 36-inch stakes are safer. Rebar is more durable than wood, of course, and has an additional advantage at dirt sets because the round metal shaft allows the trap to swivel around, keeping the trapped animal from tangling and kinking the chain.

In softer soils, especially when trapping powerful animals like coyotes, raccoons, bobcats, and otters, cross staking (driving two stakes at a

Concrete reinforcement steel, often called "rebar," makes good, durable trap stakes that can be used for many years. Even at today's high steel prices, these stakes are economical to make and use.

90-degree angle) is a good solution. This greatly increases holding power, and two 36-inch cross stakes will provide a secure anchor even in sand.

In recent years, many brands of so-called disposable stakes have become popular. These are made of a length of snare-type cable attached to a metal anchor. The cable is attached to the trap with an S-hook or other fastener, and the disposable anchor is driven into the ground with a special driver, usually a smooth, pointed piece of rebar. When the trapper gives a firm tug on the cable, the anchor turns in the soil and holds securely.

As the name suggests, these disposable stakes were designed to be left in the soil after use. However, they can usually be retrieved by using a modified car jack or pry pole. Sometimes the anchor is bent in the retrieval process, but it can be straightened and reused several times. Disposable stakes are useful in several situations, including rocky soils, water trapping, and on-foot traplines, where carrying heavy rebar stakes is a problem.

Water sets can sometimes be staked with the above methods, but most water sets call for a different strategy. In most cases, it's desirable to drown the catch quickly. Drowning is humane, it minimizes the chance of the animal escaping or being stolen, and it keeps the animal from tearing up the set.

A good drowning rig can be as simple as driving the trap stake in deeper water, using a longer chain or a length of wire to reach the desired depth. For small animals like muskrat and mink, the weight of the trap is usually sufficient to drown the animal. Driving a second stake (called a "tangle stake") partway into the bottom, so the animal will tangle the trap stake around it and be unable to return to dry land or shallow water, is a slight improvement. It's effective for muskrat, mink, and sometimes raccoon.

Disposable stakes have become popular in recent years. Usually the stake consists of an anchor that is driven into the ground, a short piece of cable, and an S-hook or other fastener for attaching the trap to the cable, similar to the one shown here laying on the log. At left is a conventional stake made of a nut welded onto a length of half-inch rebar, and next to the rebar stake is a driver for pushing the disposable anchor into the ground. A three- or four-pound hammer is the right tool for driving both types of stakes.

For larger, more powerful water animals, such as beaver and otter, a more positive drowning system is needed. An otter can be reliably held in a dry set, provided the trap is strong enough, but a beaver will almost always leave a toe or entire front foot in a foothold trap if it can't get to water and drown. And drowning the catch is desirable for otter trapping as well, for the reasons given on the preceding page.

A slide-wire drowning rig is the solution. The standard slider rig consists of two stakes connected by a sturdy wire or cable, with the trap attached to the wire with a sliding lock. The stakes are driven, one near the set and one in deeper water, with the wire stretched tight between them.

The slider itself is either a bent washer, an L-shaped piece of metal, a universal swivel, or another type of lock that moves freely along the wire in one direction (down the wire toward deeper water, naturally) but will bind on the wire when pulled in the opposite direction. When the trapped animal goes down the wire in an attempt to escape, it can't return to shore and quickly drowns. Traps are attached to the slide wires either directly or by means of an S-hook or other fastener connecting the trap chain and the slide lock.

Pre-rigging your slide-wire rigs saves time making sets and is highly recommended. I make most of my rigs about five feet long, with ten percent of them about 10 feet. These two lengths cover 99 percent of the situations on my trapline, for raccoons, mink, beaver, and otter. I use $\frac{5}{64}$ aircraft cable (the same as I use for snares) and make a tight loop on each

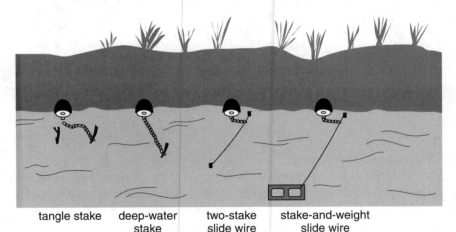

| tangle stake | deep-water stake | two-stake slide wire | stake-and-weight slide wire |

Various methods of staking drowning sets. From left: tangle stake, single deep-water stake, two-stake slide wire, and stake-and-weight slide wire.

end with a double ferrule pounded flat to hold the loop in place. The loops are about ¾-inch in diameter, big enough to accommodate a ½-inch rebar stake. On the cable between the loops is a universal swivel with S-hook attached.

When making a set, it's a quick and simple matter to uncoil the rig and clip the trap to the slider with my S-hook tool, either staking both ends of the wire or using the stake-and-weight method and attaching the weight to the lower end with a piece of wire. A disposable stake or a weight of sufficient size (sash weight, railroad tie plate, concrete block, mesh bag filled with rocks) can be used instead of the deep-water stake.

FASTENING TRAPS WITH WIRE OR CABLE

Although many inexperienced trappers use these fastening methods inappropriately and cause themselves problems in the process, using wire or cable to fasten traps to nearby objects can be effective and efficient. It's especially appropriate for many types of body-gripper trap sets, since the captured animal usually expires quickly and doesn't fight the trap much. It's also effective for trapping smaller animals such as muskrats and mink in water sets, especially when the object being wired to is in or under the water.

It's important to use a large enough cable or wire, because the trapped animal will twist and tangle it. For muskrats and mink, a single strand of 14-gauge wire or small-diameter snare cable is usually sufficient, but larger animals require more. Doubled 14-gauge wire will hold raccoon, but is probably too light for otter and beaver. Eleven gauge or even nine gauge wire is better, or a minimum cable size of ³⁄₃₂. Also, when wiring or cabling a beaver snare to a tree or bush, make sure the fastening point is at ground level or the snared beaver is likely to cut it down and escape.

Using wire or cable is most likely going to result in the destruction of your set location, so if a remake is desirable, consider another fastening option.

GRAPPLES AND DRAGS

Grapples come in many shapes and sizes, both homemade and manufactured. Their function is similar to that of a ship's anchor. The grapple has prongs that catch on brush, trees, rocks, and other obstacles when the trapped animal pulls it along.

A drag relies primarily on its own weight or shape to hinder the animal as it attempts to leave the set location after being caught. Tree limbs, sections of log, brush tops, and similar things are most often used as

Grapples are effective trap fasteners under certain trapline conditions, but looking for your trap and catch can be a time-consuming process. Make sure there's adequate brush in the set area to keep the catch from getting too far.

drags, although things like railroad tie plates, metal fence posts, lengths of pipe, old boards, and similar things can also be used.

Consider three important factors when using any drag or grapple. First, the extension chain or cable (wire is not recommended) must be long enough. Too short, and the grapple will track too straight behind the animal and won't be as likely to catch on obstacles. Five to six feet is good, but seven feet is better.

Next, the surrounding habitat must be thick enough to allow the grapple or drag to work. A grapple is useless if there's nothing for it to catch on. Drags are slightly more forgiving in this regard, but a trapped animal can go a long way with a heavy drag unless it catches on something.

Finally, when using a wooden or brush drag, be sure it's tough enough that the trapped animal won't chew it to pieces. This is especially important for coyote and raccoon.

SWIVELING
Strictly speaking, a swivel isn't a trap fastening method, but having one or more good swivels between the trap or snare and the fastening point

makes almost any fastening method more efficient. In general, the closer to the trap the swivel is placed, the more effective it will be because extension chains, cables, and wires all tend to get wrapped up eventually. The closer to the trap it is, the better a swivel will work.

In the end, how you fasten your traps is every bit as important as using the proper trap in the proper situation. Fasten them properly and you'll hold more fur, with less damage and trauma to the trapped animals. Remember, catching them is only half the battle. You also have to hold them until you return to check your traps.

4

Is "Clean" Trapping Worth the Bother?

Old-time writers of trapping books were very concerned about trapline odors and went to great lengths to make sure their sets and equipment were as odor-free as humanly possible. They boiled their traps and equipment in ashes, rinsed them in pure spring water, hung them for months from tree branches, stored them in boxes filled with pine needles, never touched them with ungloved hands. They approached water sets by getting into a stream 50 feet away from the set and wading the rest of the way, to keep from touching the bank and thereby contaminating it. They advised trappers to never wear their trapping boots in town or at the gas station, to avoid contaminating the soles. Some advised wearing a bandanna across mouth and nose, to keep from breathing on sets.

While it's a noble concept, odor-free trapping is impossible to achieve. Some of these recommendations were not only impossible; they also took up huge amounts of time and were blatant violations of the K.I.S.S. principle. Sure, it's not a good idea to deliberately contaminate sets, traps, or equipment with unnecessary foreign odors, but there's no sense being paranoid about it.

In the first place, as mentioned, there's no such thing as odorless trapping. Depending on which study you want to believe, a coyote can smell up to a million times better than a human. Whether that's accurate or not, the fact remains that coyotes, foxes, raccoons, and every other furbearer can smell far better than we can. No matter how carefully you treat and handle your traps, how nit-picky you are about keeping your footwear uncontaminated, how carefully you approach and make a set, a fox or coyote is going to know you were there. Even if a trapper executed the above things perfectly and odorlessly, the average human sheds approximately 1.5 million dead skin cells each hour. If you make a set in three minutes, that's still time enough for 75,000 cells to fall off. Unless you

Odorless trapping is a practical impossibility, but wearing gloves, minimizing disturbance at the set location, and taking other common-sense precautions all help reduce odors and improve catch rates.

wrap yourself like a mummy, some of them are going to land on the trap bed.

So what's the trapper to do? Short answer: don't worry about it too much. Here's an embarrassing but true story. In the late 1980s, I was running a predator line before work each morning. I had two sets 20 feet apart in an ideal location, on a little push-out road a few rods off the main road that cut through a rugged stretch of country, just out of sight from passing road traffic. In three days, I'd caught a coyote, a bobcat, and a gray fox there.

The fourth day, both sets were empty. That didn't bother me nearly as much as finding another trapper's fresh dirt-hole pattern directly between my two sets. There was no way he couldn't have known I was there; my catch circles were as obvious as sand traps on a golf course, and my remakes were punched into the edges of two of the circles, each with its own well-defined hole and dirt pattern. Yet there his set was, directly between my own two sets and less than a dozen feet from either of them.

It made me mad. It was public land, and he had as much right to be there as I did, but I'd beat him to the spot fair and square. And, after all, there are rules of trapline courtesy and fair play, and he'd walked all over them.

I'm ashamed to say I behaved in a less than courteous manner myself. I pulled my two sets and let the interloper have the place, but before I left, I urinated on his set—dirt pattern, backing, dirt hole, and all. I'm not proud of that, and after a couple more decades of aging and seasoning I wouldn't react that way today. But I'm glad I did it that one time, because it taught me something. When I stopped there the next morning to see if the other guy had pulled his ruined set, I found a big male gray fox bouncing around in the trap I'd watered down the previous morning.

If that doesn't illustrate that some furbearers aren't too concerned with human odors, I don't know what does. I've never forgotten that lesson. I've experimented a lot in the years since, and I can't help but come to the conclusion that, in most cases, the concept of "clean" trapping is vastly over-rated.

Clean trapping is much more important at dry sets. If you're not making first-night catches of foxes and coyotes, you're probably not trapping clean enough.

Far be it from me to question the collective knowledge and skill of those old-time trapping writers. Times were different when those guys taught themselves to trap. Furbearers were scarce, the rural human population was higher, and times were hard. A mink or coon was worth a week's wages, and every farm boy had a trapline. Long ago, an old man who had trapped in the 1930s told me that back then, if you found a set of coon tracks in the mud, there'd also be a set of bluetick hound tracks and two sets of brogan shoe tracks there, too, following it. That was probably an exaggeration, but probably not by much.

Today, furbearer populations are higher and competition is lower. Rural human populations are decreasing, and trapper numbers are, too. Because we have more animals to work with, and because the financial aspect of trapping isn't as important to us as it was to our great-grandfathers, clean trapping is simply not as important.

For one thing, clean trapping is a considerable bother, and like any bother, it slows you down. If it takes 10 minutes to make a squeaky-clean set and only five to make one that's not quite so sterile, simple mathematics shows it will take twice as long to set the same amount of traps.

You'll probably catch more fur in clean, odorless sets than in dirty, smelly ones. It's only common sense. But will that percentage double? My own experience with clean versus not-so-clean traps indicates otherwise. The bottom line is inescapable: if you're too persnickety and fussy about making sure everything is clean as a whistle, it's going to take more time and you won't be able to maintain as many sets. In the end you'll catch less fur, not more.

COMPROMISE IS THE TICKET

Don't think from what you've read so far in this chapter that it's okay to keep your traps in the grease pit of an auto repair garage between seasons. However, you don't have to be as careful about contamination as those old-time trappers (and more than a few modern-day ones) would have you think.

Many trappers believe waxing traps is the ultimate deodorizing treatment. But that's silly. Wax itself, even clean wax, has an odor, and if the human nose can detect it, you can bet a furbearer can. Also, since the wax picks up odors from its surroundings, it's going to carry trace scents—your breath, the sweat that seeps through your "clean" cotton gloves, the rusty spots in the bed of your pickup, the muskrat you carelessly let brush against the trap at a previous stop earlier in the day . . . in short, almost anything in the environment.

The objective is to have traps that aren't heavily contaminated with human scent or anything else. One of the surest ways to not catch an animal is to spill some lure or bait on the trap itself. A fox, coyote, or coon will almost certainly dig up the trap, and diggers rarely get caught. Once that animal learns there's likely to be a funny-shaped metal object in the ground in front of a hole with that particular smell coming out of it, you've created a "trap-shy" animal, although he's never had a pinched foot. He's not scared of the trap because he doesn't know what it is. But he'll dig it up all the same.

For what it's worth, here's how I deal with the odor issue: First, I clean and treat my traps and equipment as described in the previous chapter. After they're treated, I store them in a small room in my fur shed, in a different part of the building from where I skin and stretch my fur. The traps are stored in plastic carrying crates or hung in bundles from the wall.

Minimizing odors at set locations is a good idea, but it can be taken to extremes that are detrimental rather than helpful. If it takes twice as long to make a clean set as one that's not quite so clean, the trade-off may not be worth it. Do what you can to minimize odors, but don't get so paranoid about it that it cripples your operation.

When I'm setting traps, I try to handle them as little as possible with bare hands, but I'm not paranoid about it. If I need to touch a trap and my gloves aren't handy, I won't interrupt the routine or go to the extra trouble of putting on the gloves—but neither will I bare-hand the trap any more than necessary. I always make sets without a kneeling cloth, because set-making is faster that way. I also use bare hands to apply lure, bait, and urine because it's likewise faster and also because lure or bait easily contaminates your gloves, which contaminates your traps, which causes critters to dig them up.

But I try not to be careless. To minimize odor, I don't spend more time at the set than necessary. (I'd do this anyway, because of the efficiency factor.) I don't spit or pee or blow my nose near the set, despite the story related at the beginning of this chapter. If I get lure or bait or urine on my hands, I wash them before making another dry set. I'll sometimes remake a set after a catch using the same trap, because the furbearer's odor has already saturated the set area and the trap won't smell any different than its surroundings. However, when I pull a trap that's caught a furbearer, I won't use that trap at another dry set before it's treated again, because at a new set its odor would make it stand out.

I am aware that my casual attitude toward foreign odors on the trapline causes me to miss a few smart, old, toe-pinched furbearers every year. But a trapper needs to leave some furbearers for seed, anyway, so why not let the smart ones be the breeding stock? Those dumb ones are just as valuable, and they're not so much trouble to catch. While some other odor-paranoid trapper is out there poking along, taking all those extra precautions to keep things as odor-free as he can possibly make them, I'll be running twice as many sets and catching way more fur.

Don't be sloppy. But don't be foolish, either.

5

The Basics of Eye Appeal

I was in Kansas, accompanying a friend on his High Plains coyote line. We were driving between a wheat field and a CRP pasture, and as we topped a rise we could see the next set location at the bottom of the grade. Boy, oh boy, could we see it. It looked like a miniature backhoe had been at work down there. And in a way, I suppose that was true.

"What . . . ?"

"Badger," my buddy J. R. replied. "They do that."

Sure enough, as we got closer we could see him peering at us over the rim of the fort of prairie loam he'd pulled into the set, reaching as far as he could in all directions and raking dirt toward him.

Badgers are about as common as unicorns in the country where I learned to trap, and I was goggle-eyed as I examined the perfectly formed circle of soil surrounded by its shallow moat, with the furious badger hissing and snarling from its center.

J. R. quickly dispatched the badger and pulled the trap, but he surprised me when he laid the animal in the truck and came out with his set-making bucket and three clean traps. He must have seen the questioning look in my eye.

"Coons," he explained. "We've got a lot of 'em, but out in the middle of this wide-open country, there aren't many places to make high-percentage coons sets. We don't have many terrain features to funnel their movements, so they're liable to wander anywhere. But they'll come investigate this thing." He pointed at the badger moat.

"Coyotes and foxes will come, too," J. R. said, "but a badger catch site is a real magnet for open-country coons. I never fail to set one up." In ten minutes we were on our way, leaving three dirt-hole sets ringing the circle of earth.

It made sense. Back home, I'd learned that the most productive coon sets were the ones that had eye appeal, the ones that gave passing raccoons a reason to mosey over and poke around. In that featureless landscape, where J. R. (who owns more than 20,000 acres) had the previous

The generic predator set, because of its inconspicuous nature, is an excellent choice where theft or interference by other humans is a possibility, but it must be made right on the travelway or at a location with eye appeal. This set is at the end of the log, and the log serves as an attractor for cats and canines traveling the road through these open woods.

morning pointed out a scraggly elm in an arroyo and said, "There's my tree," any land feature at all would have eye appeal.

If ever there was a furbearer whose personality made it susceptible to flamboyant set-making, it's ol' Brer Coon. He finds his food mostly with his nose and his sensitive front feet, but it's his eyes that tell him where to smell and feel around. The savvy trapper knows this and takes advantage of it at every opportunity. It works in all types of raccoon habitat, from shorelines to ridgetops, from Canada to Texas, and from California to Maine.

However, eye appeal sets aren't limited to coons. Foxes, coyotes, bobcats, mink, beavers, otters, muskrats—in fact, every species of furbearer, as far as I've been able to determine—are suckers for sets with eye appeal.

TWO TYPES OF EYE APPEAL

The first type of eye appeal, and the most common, is where the eye appeal is natural. In this type, the trapper makes a set near an object on the trapline that stands out from its surroundings, depending on the

The eye appeal of this old stump at the edge of a marshy lake is undeniable. Over a four-year period before the landowner removed the stump, the author and his trapping partner caught more than fifty furbearers here— mostly muskrats, mink, and raccoons, but also two bobcats and one red fox.

object itself to draw the furbearer in. Once there, the animal finds the trapper's set and, if all goes well, gets caught.

There are two advantages to natural eye appeal sets. One is that furbearers already know the whereabouts of the object creating the eye appeal, and if the object is in a good location, they're already visiting it. The other advantage is that making sets at natural eye appeal locations is quicker, since the trapper doesn't have to spend time creating something that will catch the critter's eye. Therefore, natural eye appeal sets are K.I.S.S. sets. Usually, a blind set or dirt-hole is adequate to catch the animal after the natural eye appeal of the set location draws the animal in.

It's easy to find these natural locations, because the human eye is attracted to them as well. Experience and practice help, of course, and veteran trappers can spot these locations as far away as they can see them.

"It's like there's a blinking light there, telling me where to set," an old trapper told me many years ago, when, as an inexperienced youngster, I asked why he'd made a particular set. The location was a lone rock along a sandy stream bank, and I found the old trapper's set because there was a drowned mink in it. He came along about the same time I did, and I asked the question because I'd gone by that rock without a second glance, never dreaming it was a hotspot.

I wasn't satisfied with his answer at the time, but now I understand it. The old trapper was right; once the eye is trained to look for these places, they do seem to jump out at you. Depending on the targeted species, natural eye appeal set locations are as varied as the species themselves. But they have one thing in common: they're noticeable, and the best locations are usually noticeable from a distance.

If you still don't understand the concept, here's something that might help. When you first approach an area to set traps, try not to look at the general area until you get into a position where you can see the whole place at once, or at least as much of the area as possible. Look at the ground in front of your feet, then raise your head and try to take in the whole area at once. Whatever catches your eye first is probably going to be the best location to make a natural eye appeal set—log, rock, beaver dam, lone tree in a pasture, brushy area along a bare stream bank (or, conversely, an open area along an otherwise brushy bank). In short, anything that's different.

Eye appeal can be simply defined as the first thing that catches your eye when you look at a potential set location. Go to the object that first catches your eye, and chances are there will be good set-making opportunities there.

That's all natural eye appeal is—something that stands out from its surroundings. Once you've made sets at a few of these locations and caught a few furbearers there, those lights will start blinking for you, too.

ARTIFICIAL EYE APPEAL

Sometimes, though, there won't be any blinking lights. This is especially true in flat, open farmland or prairie territory, but it also happens along streams, farm roads, and other places where furbearers travel but there's nothing to attract their attention. These places are good set locations, but they sometimes need a little help.

That's where manmade eye appeal comes in, and it can be just as varied as the things that have natural eye appeal. Manmade eye appeal sets are discussed in the following chapters, but here are a few examples: making large, conspicuous dirt holes or large dirt patterns for predator trapping; hanging feathers, surveyor's tape, or similar things as attention-catching flags over or near sets made for bobcats; remaking dry-land sets at the edge of catch circles after removing a catch; and using extra-large pocket sets (dry or wet) for raccoon trapping.

In every instance, the objective is to catch the animal's attention from a distance and draw it closer until it can smell the bait or lure or be otherwise enticed to investigate the set closely enough to be caught. A visual long-distance call lure, you might say.

CONSIDER THE POSSIBILITIES

Not every set location calls for eye appeal. In fact, sometimes adding any kind of visuals can work against you. For example, if you're making a set at a natural bottleneck in a trail, such as a fence crawl-through, you don't want the target animal to alter its travel route or slow down. You want it to hit your trap or snare at a normal angle and speed. Ditto with swim-through sets, which will be discussed in the chapters on beaver, otter, mink, and muskrats.

But aside from these situations, most good set locations depend to some extent on eye appeal, either natural or manmade, and examples of this can get pretty wacky sometimes. One stop on my predator line, for example, uses as its eye appeal a discarded white porcelain American Standard commode. It sits upright beside an ATV trail that receives heavy use in deer season, but almost none during trapping season. It's on a little rise at a bend in the trail, both of which are helpful, but it's the throne that's the attractor, and I routinely catch two or three predators there every season, mostly coyotes but also gray foxes, bobcats, and coons.

Some set locations provide both eye appeal and a natural narrowing of a travelway, such as this log at the water's edge.

I don't recommend dumping commodes in the woods so you can set traps around them, but that toilet is one of my better set locations, even though the aesthetics of the situation leave something to be desired. I've also successfully used other discarded stuff for eye appeal—old coils of barbed wire, abandoned vehicles, even an old rusted-out double-bed box spring.

The point is there's practically no limit to the things a trapper can use for eye appeal, both natural and manmade. Keep the eye appeal factor in mind as you read the chapters on trapping the various furbearers and see how often it comes into play. You can't help but notice how variable this concept of eye appeal really is.

Just to show you how well it works: Remember the three sets my Kansas buddy J. R. made around the badger moat? The next morning, we took three big prairie coons out of them.

6

Scouting and Other Pre-Season Preparation

The more an athletic coach knows about his opponents, the better off he is, and the more likely he is to formulate a winning game plan. That's why coaches from junior high through the pros rely on scouting reports.

The same principle carries over into outdoor activities. The best anglers on a given lake will be the ones who spend a lot of time on the water, learning the lake and how to fish it. The best deer or turkey hunters are the ones who spend a lot of time in the woods, both during the season and when the season is closed. And the best trappers are the ones who know their traplines best.

A lot of this intimate knowledge accumulates from the simple act of trapping an area for several years. Whether you make an effort to learn things or not, some of it inevitably soaks in. But no matter how long a trapper works the same territory, things are going to change from year to year. It can be a costly mistake to assume that last year's observations and experiences tell you everything you need to know about your trapline for this year.

Of course, scouting takes time, and, in these days of high fuel prices, extra trips over the trapline can get expensive in a hurry. Consequently, not many trappers scout their trapping territory as well as they should. But even a little bit of scouting helps. In fact, after an observant trapper has worked the same area for several years, a little bit of scouting may be all he needs.

POST-SEASON SCOUTING

When the season closes, most of us are ready for a break. Bodies and equipment are frazzled, hands are sore and chapped, and we're tired. But a week or two later, after a good rest, is a prime time to go take a look at that new section of country you've been thinking about moving into. Late February and early March usually see a lot of furbearer movement, especially south of the Snow Belt, and it's a good time to look for sign since the vegetation hasn't started growing yet.

It's wise to make notes during this post-season run, especially if you're looking at new country. It's a long time between late winter and the start of the next trapping season, and if your memory is anything like mine, it's going to need all the help you can give it.

You don't have to go into great detail. I usually make my scouting notes directly on my maps, using letters or numbers as symbols to indicate what kind of sign I've found, and underlines or circles to denote especially promising areas. Then I pretty much forget about my trapline until early fall.

MAPS

Speaking of maps, here's a guarantee: no matter how long you've trapped the same area, and no matter how well you think you know that area, you do not know as much about it as a topographical map does. An hour of studying—not just looking at, but studying—topo maps of your trapping country will show you things you'd never learn in fifty years of driving the roads, floating the streams, and traipsing through the landscape on foot. Topographical maps are to effective trapline scouting what the old-time Indian scouts were to wagon trains. Except infinitely better.

No trapper's equipment inventory is complete without a few maps of his trapping territory.

Standard topographic maps have good detail and are valuable trapline tools, but their large size makes them unwieldy for in-the-field use.

The U.S. Geological Survey produces topographical maps. They are for sale to the public through the mail or at a wide variety of government offices and private businesses, from state geological survey offices to county NRCS offices to sporting goods stores. The USGS provides free index maps for each state, available on request, and individual topo maps are ordered by name from the index map. For state index maps, contact the U.S. Geological Survey, 1-888-275-8747, www.usgs.gov.

Regardless the furbearers you're after, the detail contained on a topo map will allow you to identify and pinpoint likely travelways, crossroads, concentration points, and denning or feeding areas. Furthermore, the topos will show you where these potential hotspots lie in relation to each other and the logical routes to get from one to the next to the next. Topo maps are available in several scales, but the 1:24,000 series (also known as the 7½-minute series) is the most useful to trappers. On these maps, an inch equals 2,000 feet, or about 0.4 miles.

One of the biggest problems with topos is their unwieldiness. A 7½-minute map measures 22 by 27 inches, which is fine on the dining room table but pretty hard to use in the cab of your truck. Another potential problem with topos is their cost, which as of March 2007 was $6 per map. A single 7½-minute topo covers a chunk of land roughly 9½ miles deep by 7¾ miles wide, approximately 73 square miles. If you have a small trapline and it happens to lie near the center of a topo map's cover-

CD AND ONLINE MAP COMPANIES

Maptech, Inc.
www.maptech.com
888-839-5551
Product: Terrain Navigator

iGage Mapping Corporation
www.igage.com
1-888-450-4922
Product: All Topo Maps

Maps a la carte, Inc.
www.topozone.com
Fax: 978-251-1396
Product: TopoZone

DeLorme
www.delorme.com
888-839-5551
Product: TopoUSA

There are also alternatives for the less computer-literate. Many state wildlife agencies (Arkansas, Kansas, and Nebraska, for example) publish outdoor atlases, which are large-format books of county maps with public areas shown on them. While these lack the topographic detail that's so helpful for armchair scouting, they partially make up for this deficiency by being affordable (usually around $20) and handy to use. They're excellent tools for planning a trapline route around the countryside.

Similarly, DeLorme also publishes a series of state atlas books in addition to its electronic products. While these maps have some topographical relief and other features of interest to trappers, the scale is so small (1:400,000, or about six miles to the inch) that this information isn't all that useful. But like the county atlases, these books are valuable for mapping out a trapline route, and they're available for all states.

age, you may only need to buy a single map. Usually, though, even a small trapline will lap over into two or more maps, and longline trappers may need a dozen or more to cover their lines. Not only does this get expensive in a hurry, but it also compounds the unwieldiness factor.

There are other options. Several companies produce electronic versions of topographical maps, available on the Internet or on CDs. Some companies offer maps state by state, while others have larger geographic coverage but usually less detail. The initial cost is often higher than paper maps, but in the long run these products are cheaper because their coverage equals hundreds, if not thousands, of topo sheets. These maps are printable from your computer screen, and they're seamless. In other words, you can make any point the center of a map. These electronic maps are limited to the paper size of your printer (usually 8½ x 11 inches), so they don't cover as much territory at the same scale as a standard topo. But neither do they fill up a truck cab when you're looking at them, and a trapper can string together a customized set of maps that precisely fit his trapline. Carry a set of these in a ring binder in clear plastic sleeves, and you have the ultimate trapline map.

WHAT ARE YOU LOOKING FOR?

Having maps is one thing. Knowing how to pull information out of them is another. However, it's not a hard skill to learn. Stream drainages, marshes, springs, and other water features are all shown on topographical maps, and these can be hotspot set locations for water and land animals alike. Other things to look for include boundary lines between cover types, treelines or woodlots separating open areas, sharp horseshoe bends and the resulting peninsulas in streams, bridges, stream junctions, forest trails or unimproved roads, steep bluffs or cliffs, low saddles on ridgelines, lake or pond outlets, points of timber sticking out into fields, and

It doesn't matter how long you've been trapping an area and how well you think you know it, you don't know it as well as a topo map does.

similar features that might focus or funnel the movements of furbearers. It's a lot easier to find these things on maps than on the ground.

Also, look for potential travelways connecting two or more likely pieces of furbearer habitat. For example, a small creek that drains a group of manmade catfish ponds and runs into a larger creek or river a mile or two downstream may well be a hotspot travelway for mink, otters, raccoons, and other furbearers. A fenceline or treeline through open farm or pasture land and connecting two 40-acre woodlots may be a super highway for raccoons, cats, and canines. A two-track road through a large block of timber may serve as a travelway for a whole host of upland furbearers.

Find a good bunch of these terrain features and mark them on your maps, then get out there on the ground and check a few of them out. That's the only way to find out if furbearers are actually present in worthwhile numbers. However, once you become skilled at knowing what to look for on your maps, you'll be surprised at how high your percentage will be.

GETTING PERMISSION TO TRAP PRIVATE LAND

It's possible to run a very productive trapline on public land, but trapping private land offers the advantage of added security for your sets and catches. Getting permission to trap isn't all that difficult, provided you use common sense and the basic rules of courtesy when asking.

Here are a few tips to increase your chances of success: First, try to find out the landowner's name before you visit. County courthouses maintain property ownership maps (called plat maps) for sale or inspection, usually in the County Clerk's office. Knowing the person's name is an important first step to making a good impression.

By all means, ask permission in person. It's all too easy for the landowner to brush you off when you try it by phone. Dress well. Not necessarily in your Sunday best, but not in your trapping clothes, either. Dress neatly and conservatively, the way you'd dress if you were taking your family out to a restaurant and a movie. Trapping is dirty, muddy, bloody business, and while it's understandable and appropriate for us to wear old clothes on the trapline, it pays to clean up a little before asking a landowner's permission to trap. You wouldn't want someone who looks like a hobo knocking on your door, and the landowner doesn't, either.

Try to catch the landowner when he or she isn't busy, and never knock on the door at mealtime. Introduce yourself as soon as the landowner comes to the door, and offer a business card if you have one. (If you don't, getting some printed is a good investment.) Be polite, and get

Asking landowners for permission to trap is an uncomfortable prospect for many trappers, but it can lead to good trapping opportunities for years to come.

to the point. Tell the landowner your purpose for visiting, and mention up front the species you want to trap. Mention of the words beaver and coyote are often all it takes to get in the pasture gate.

Bring a trap or two with you for show-and-tell purposes, but don't carry them to the front door. Many people are totally unfamiliar with modern steel traps, and they think all traps are huge, toothy contraptions. When they're shown a 1½ coilspring, a snare, or other modern tool of the trade, it often means the difference between yes and no. I sometimes set a foothold trap and spring it on my hand, to demonstrate that it doesn't cut off an animal's foot. It's a silly trick, but it works wonders.

Promise to treat the landowner's property with respect, and if permission to trap is granted, keep that promise. Before you leave the landowner's doorstep, make sure you know the ground rules. Stay off farm roads when they're wet and subject to be rutted up, close gates behind you, don't litter. These are all common-sense rules, but they're all very important.

After the season, send the landowner a thank-you note or make another visit to say thanks, and let the landowner know what you caught off the property. It's not a bad idea to send or deliver a small gift if you can afford it, and this doesn't have to amount to much to make a good impression. One of my favorite post-season gifts for my landowners is a small container of cooking seasoning that's manufactured in my home state. A container of this stuff costs about a dollar, and the goodwill it generates is priceless.

Once you get your foot in the door with several landowners and demonstrate your trustworthiness, word will spread. You'll soon have landowners calling you, and even if they don't, they'll probably have heard of you from their neighbors and permission will be easier to get.

THE PRE-SEASON CHECK

Whether you trap public land, private land, or both, it's always a good idea to make one quick run over at least a representative part of your trapline not long before the season opens. Running the entire line is the best option, because manmade changes and natural events like drought, flooding, fires, and storms can drastically alter the quality and type of habitat in an area over the course of a summer. This in turn can have an effect—good or bad—on the number of furbearers that habitat will support.

No matter if the changes are good or bad, it's helpful to know about them before steel-stringing time. It won't do you any good to carry a peach basket full of muskrat traps to that marsh you trapped last year if the farmer drained the marsh over the summer—or, almost as bad, if disease got into the 'rat population and wiped them out. And if that snaggy old 40-acre patch of woods where you caught so many coons last year has been cleared for the latest Wal-Mart, it's best to know that before the season starts so you can make other plans.

Refer to your post-season trapping notes, and revisit those places where you noted good furbearer sign or good-looking habitat. Make up-to-date notations as you learn what's going on at each place. Then, between this final scouting trip and Opening Day, make any revisions necessary to your trapline route and strategy. Then wait for the big day, get a good night's sleep, and hit it with everything you've got.

7

Maximizing Your Efficiency

Few sayings are more shopworn than this one: time is money. Few sayings are more accurate, either. Time *is* money, on the trapline or anywhere else. The more of it you have to devote to trapping, the more fur you're going to catch.

The problem, of course, is that there's only so much time available. Most trappers have jobs, other hobbies or interests, and families, and these things cut into the number of hours available for the trapline. The clock and the calendar limit even full-time, hard-rolling professional longliners. There are only twenty-four hours in the day, and even the toughest longliner has to eat and sleep.

That's why getting up to speed at the beginning of your trapping season is so important, whether you're going to trap for a weekend or for three months, whether your trapline is a dozen sets along the creek behind the house or 250 sets spread over three counties. The quicker you can get your sets out, the more sets you can make and the more trap-nights you'll have . . . and the bigger your fur check will be when it's all over.

There's the competition factor, too. Other trappers are after those same furbearers, and other things being equal, he who gets there firstest with the mostest will catch the most fur. In the northern states, severe weather can also be a critical factor. The arrival of cold weather and heavy snow and ice cover effectively ends trapping season for many folks, and they have to make fur while the sun shines.

Okay, those are the reasons for getting up to speed as quickly as possible when the season opens. They're valid. They're not arguable. But how do you go about it?

PRE-SEASON PREPARATION
Getting up to speed starts long before opening day. All your equipment should be cleaned, repaired, sorted, and ready to go. Opening day eve is no time to be knocking rust and mud off a tangled pile of dirty traps.

The more time a trapper spends on the line, the more fur he will catch. This is true regardless of skill level.

And you should have long since done the scouting, permission gathering, equipment buying, and all those other things that make the difference between success and failure.

But beyond buying supplies, getting your traps in good shape, and scouting your line, there are many other little things you can do before the season to speed things up on those all-important first couple days.

Bait Gathering

Some trappers use bait at every set, while other trappers don't use it at all. Most of us fall somewhere in between. Regardless of how much or how little bait you plan to use on your line, though, have it on hand before it's time to start setting.

If you bait with fish, save fish heads, entrails, and carcasses after they've been filleted, and freeze them in convenience-size packages. If you hunt squirrels, rabbits, quail, pheasants, or other small game, freeze the unwanted parts of these as well. A few mousetraps kept baited around a barn or grain storage area can give you enough mice and other small rodents and voles to bait a heck of a lot of dirt-hole sets. So can

The heads, skins, and entrails of squirrels, ducks, and other small game bagged during hunting season can be used for bait at sets during trapping season. Check state regulations first.

picking up fresh road kills as opportunity arises. Save old cooking grease and mix it with cracklings, crisp-fried bacon pieces, cheap raspberry jelly, sardine oil, or other similar things to make effective paste bait or trailing scent for coons and other animals. Or, find a commercial fisherman or fish market in your area and buy cheap, oily fish such as carp, gar, or buffalo and cut them into chunks before freezing.

Trap Stakes and Drags
If you use wooden stakes on your line (good for many water trapping situations, but usually not for dry-land trapping), make sure you have an adequate supply before the season. Hardwood tree limbs or saplings such as persimmon and hickory make excellent trap stakes, but they're much better if they're cut in spring or summer and allowed to season for a few months before using them. Either buy rebar stakes or make more to replace any lost or bent during the previous season.

Likewise, if you plan to use many brush drags on your line, cut these ahead of time and have them already in place at the set locations where you're going to need them. Wandering around looking for a dead limb to use as a drag is a poor use of your time on opening day.

If you use sliding-wire rigs for drowning sets, have a good supply pre-rigged and ready to go so all you need to do is stake them in place and use an S-hook to attach the trap. Building slide-wire setups one at a time on the trapline eats up huge amounts of time. In fact, installing a pre-rigged slide-wire rig at a set location is pretty time consuming, so if you can, make a trip over your line just before opening day to pre-install at least some of your slide wires. This speeds things up on opening day.

Look to Your Wheels

Service your trapline vehicle before the season opens. The closer to the opener you can accomplish this chore, the better. This is especially true if you put a lot of miles on your rig during the season. Trapping is hard on a vehicle.

Change the oil and filters, of course, but also don't forget a lube job, belts and hoses, and fluid levels. Make sure your tires are sound, fully inflated and balanced, and make sure also your front end is aligned. Check the ball joints and universal joints for soundness and wear.

Make sure your spare tire is good and is fully inflated. Carrying two spares isn't a bad idea, since many trapline miles are pretty rough and

Pre-making a supply of slide-wire drowners in various lengths is a real time-saver on the trapline.

Keeping your trapline vehicle organized helps keep your equipment clean, saves time, and in general makes for a more efficient operation.

you're often far from the nearest tire shop. With two spares, you can keep rolling if you have a flat, without having to worry about taking time out to get the spare fixed.

OPENING DAY EVE

Finally, all the nit-picky pre-season stuff is behind you, and it's time to load the truck. Don't think you can run out while the 10 o'clock news is on the night before the season and throw all your stuff in. Do it that way and you'll pay the price the next day in inefficiency and left-behind items. Loading your rig isn't an all-day job if you've done your pre-season work well, but it does take an hour or so to do it right, and it's a job best tackled in daylight.

Make a list of the things you're going to need on the first setting day, and check off the items as you load them. Organization is important, so give some thought to how you organize your vehicle so you can find and reach what you need easily and quickly.

Be realistic about how many traps, stakes, drags, and other gear you take for the first day's setting. Sure, carry enough hardware so you don't run short, but there's no sense loading two hundred traps when you know you'll be hard-pressed to make a third that many sets. The extras only get in the way and slow you down. Carry only what you think you'll need, plus a few extras for a cushion. Load more traps as needed after the first day of setting.

Last but not least, carry plenty of drinking water and high-energy, easy-to-eat foods—candy or granola bars, raisins, peanuts, oranges, jerky, a sandwich or two. You don't have time to stop at a restaurant or convenience store, and you'll need energy before day's end.

DAY ONE

Try to get as much rest as possible the night before. In some states, legal setting time comes at midnight, and some eager trappers are out there at 12:01 A.M., making sets by flashlight. Do that if you're so minded, but getting a crack-of-dawn start has always made more sense to me because you begin the day with a good night's rest, and it's a lot faster and easier to make sets by daylight anyway. In my state, legal setting time begins at sunrise. When the legal minute comes, I'm standing at my first set location with a trap in my hand.

Develop a system and stick with it. I carry traps, stakes, and other stuff in a five-gallon plastic bucket fitted with a canvas liner with pouches. Lures, baits, and urines go in the outside pouches to minimize the risk of contaminating my traps, sifter, and digging tools.

Other trappers use pack baskets to haul stuff to set locations. At least two manufacturers make a sort of open-topped gym bag for trapline use,

A set-making container of some kind is essential for running a smooth trapline. A five-gallon bucket makes a serviceable container and is easily cleaned if it becomes contaminated.

big enough to carry a couple traps and stakes plus tools needed to make sets. Find something that works for you, then customize it and stick with it. It'll make your life simpler, and your trapline faster and more efficient.

Carry everything you think you'll need when you leave the truck at each stop so you won't waste time making return trips to the vehicle. However, don't load yourself down unnecessarily. If you're trapping foxes and cats in upland habitat, you'll probably be making no more than two or three sets per stop, so carry enough hardware for those sets and no more.

Back at the vehicle, replenish the traps and equipment in your carrying receptacle before driving to the next stop. That way, the amount of hardware you just used will be fresh in your mind, and you won't forget to add more traps when you arrive at the next location.

AT THE END OF THE DAY

You'll be tired at the end of the first trapline day, regardless whether your line is short or long, regardless whether you're in good shape or not. Trapping is strenuous business, and the first few days are the toughest. Still, don't neglect to do the things that will make you ready to go tomorrow.

Top off your fuel tank, and replenish any needed supplies—traps, wire, lures, whatever—before you go into the house. Trust me, it's much harder to come back outside and do these chores after you've been in where it's warm and comfortable and smells like supper.

After tomorrow's supplies are laid in, go get a hot shower and a hot meal and, again, get as much rest as you can. Because as tiring as the first setting day can be, it's almost never as tiring as the first check day. In addition to running your existing sets and adding more, you're going to have some furbearers to process.

IT'S ABOUT SAVING SECONDS, NOT MINUTES

Keep in mind: you're not looking for ways to save big hunks of time. The important thing is finding ways to shave ten seconds off making a set at Point A and five more seconds down the road at Point B. Don't backtrack, don't waste motion, don't take five steps when three will do. Don't dawdle.

Before long, this sort of trapline attitude and behavior becomes second nature, and those little fractions of minutes start to add up. Do it all day long, and by the time you reach Point ZZ, you'll have saved a couple hours. You can do a lot with a chunk of time that big.

8

Priceless Tips for the Trapper

This chapter is lagniappe, a little something extra—a collection of time-saving or money-saving tips (which are one and the same), presented in no particular order. Some are repetitions or restatements of things said elsewhere in this book, and some are being said here for the first time:

• When coilspring traps start to weaken, replace the springs with new ones designed for a larger trap. For example, put number 3 springs in number 1¾ traps, and 1¾ springs in 1½s. This gives traps more strength and speed than they had when new, and the extra strength and speed helps get a firmer, higher grip on an animal's foot and prevents the foot from sliding or turning inside the trap jaws—the primary cause of foot damage.

• Dilute your trap dip beyond the manufacturer's recommendation. Adding about 25 to 30 percent more thinner (unleaded gasoline or lantern fuel) is about right. The manufacturers are in the business to sell products, and their standard recommendation produces a thick mixture that leaves too thick a coating on the steel.

• Loop your body-gripper triggers with wire or monofilament fishing line to keep animals from slipping through the traps or getting caught too far back on the body.

• Use eye appeal at your sets at every opportunity to increase the chances of visits from furbearers.
When waxing traps, also wax the top six or eight inches of your metal trap stakes. The wax helps deodorize and protect the steel and also helps lubricate the swiveling action between the stake and the trap swivel.

• Wax your rolls of trapper tie wire also. They won't rust if waxed, and the wax helps bind the wires together so you won't get those maddening snarls of wire peeling off the roll all the time.

• If you use commercially prepared baits and lures, wrap clear tape around the bottles to cover the labels so you can still read them after

Upgrading the springs on coilspring traps is an excellent way to make them faster and stronger, and it can be done very easily with a minimum of tools. A thin-bladed screwdriver and a pair of pliers are all you need.

they've been used and repeatedly gotten wet and muddy. If you make your own lures and baits, mark the containers so you can tell what's what.

• Make sure you have spares of critical equipment such as pliers, hatchet, dirt sifter, gloves, and the like, in case of breakage or loss.

• Be as consistent as possible in your set making. You don't need a lot of fancy sets for most trapline situations, so develop a repertoire of favored sets and stick with them. You'll get faster and more efficient by keeping it simple and consistent. Being fast saves time, and time is money.

• Make up a good supply of slide-wire drowning rigs during the off-season, to speed up set making when it's trapping time.

• Do things the same way every time. When you approach a set location, lay your equipment down in the same place relative to the set. That way, you won't have to look for it or grope around for it. For example, at dirt-hole sets, a right-handed trapper would probably be best served by putting his set-making bucket on the right side of the set-making spot, so he can reach his equipment with a minimum of bother and strain. Like-wise, when you finish digging the trap bed, get in the habit of laying your sifter and digging tool in the same place relative to the trap bed, and do it that way every time. Keep your lures in the same place. Keep your gloves and other equipment in the same place. Soon, you'll develop muscle memory and will do things subconsciously—and save even more precious trapline time.

• Because raccoons and other furbearers often travel in groups, the wise trapper employs gang-setting techniques, making several sets in a small area. This is especially important if you're only going to be in an area a short while, because once a trap has made a catch, it's out of commission until you remove the catch and remake the set.

• Use different lures at each set when you're gang setting, or, at least, throw in a change-up lure every once in a while.

• Use a trap and fastening method suitable for the largest species you're likely to catch. In most of the country, this will be a coyote.

• Watch the weather. If there's a storm coming, make an extra effort to get everything in good shape on your line, because furbearers move a lot before and during the storm, and you need to be ready for it.

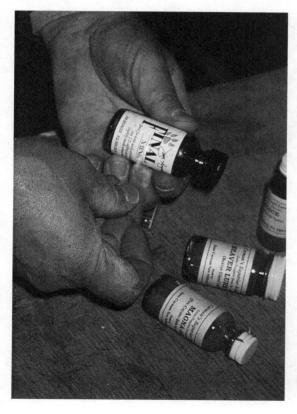

Wrap clear tape around your lure bottle labels, or you'll be guessing later at what lure you're using.

Don't be in too big a hurry to pull sets made for mink and otter. Sometimes these animals take a long time to return to an area.

• Don't trap a location too long for upland predators. If you haven't made a catch in four or five days, you probably did something wrong. Maybe there aren't any furbearers using that particular location, or maybe they've been fooled with before and are trap-shy. Or maybe your technique is sloppy or inappropriate for the conditions. Whatever the problem is, keeping your traps there a long time isn't going to fix it. The best strategy is to trap an area five to seven days and move those traps to a new location.

• The above tip also applies to beaver, muskrat, and water-based coon trapping, but not for mink and otters. In many cases, mink and otters take longer to return to a given area because of their travel habits. Often, a good mink or otter set on the first day of the season will still be a good set two months later.

• When blind setting for furbearers, it's often necessary to use guide sticks and other objects to narrow your target's travelway and guide its foot onto the trap pan, or its body through your body-gripper. However, don't be too heavy-handed. Suggest, rather than demand, that the animal go this way or that, and you'll be ahead of the game. Make it easier for the animal to go over or through the trap than around it, and that's what it will do.

• Precise set location is critical, for lured or baited sets as well as for blind sets. If you depend on lure or bait to pull an animal more than four or five feet off its intended travelway, you're asking too much.

• When using buckets or footholds for coons, use fish oil, old cooking oil, and similar cheap oil in a squirt bottle to lay down a scent trail leading to your set. Coons are exceptions to the above rule in that they can be pulled off a high bank to the water line, or vice versa, with a line of fish oil squirted along the ground.

• Empty 35mm film canisters are handy trapline items. They work very well as water-resistant lure or liquid bait holders when stuffed with a small wad of cotton, moss, or dry grass, and can be made up ahead of time, capped, and carried into the field for use. Film canisters are also good for carrying a few extra trap tags, small nails, .22 ammo, aspirin, salt and pepper, dry matches, and a hundred other items you often need on the trapline. Label each canister to save time.

Small trapline items like tacks, .22 ammo, trap tags, and medicine can be easily and conveniently carried in labeled 35mm film canisters.

• Besides cotton balls, moss, and balls of dried grass, other effective lure holders are small pieces of dry, porous wood; dried feet from a previously-skinned animal; bits of rabbit or muskrat fur; pieces of dried scat from your target animal; feathers; small mussel shells; and hickory nut shells or shell coverings.

• Cover your bait at all sets. Not only is this the law in most states, it's also more natural and arouses more of a furbearer's curiosity.

• If you wear glasses while running your traps, use a strap to keep them from falling off. Trappers look down a lot, and often they're in thick brush or cover to boot. A strap can save a costly pair of specs and prevent a lot of inconvenience.

• When you remove a wet mink, coon, muskrat, or opossum from a water set, snap or shake as much water as possible from the fur, then wrap the animal in several thicknesses of old newspaper and leave it wrapped while you continue to run your line. The porous paper wicks away most of the moisture and greatly speeds up the drying process.

• If you don't have time to finish all your skinning in one day, lay your remaining catch belly-down on a concrete floor. The cool concrete retards spoilage in the soft belly area.

• If you normally run your trapline early in the morning, try running at midday or in the afternoon on occasion. Run your line at night occasionally, or run the line backwards. Not only does this help break the monotony and keep your interest level high, but it also lets you view your line under different lighting conditions and from different perspectives. You'll see things you might otherwise miss. Sometimes a good set location you've been driving by will jump out at you the first time you run your line a different way.

• Keep a trapline notebook. Record set locations, catches, weather, lures and baits used, and other pertinent information. Over the length of a season and over the course of several seasons, keeping notes will help you identify trends and patterns that might otherwise escape your notice. Also, a notebook can be invaluable in showing someone else where your sets are, in case an illness, injury, or family emergency keeps you away from your trapline.

• Keep a dry change of clothes—including underwear, socks, and shoes—in a sealed plastic bag or gym bag in your trapline vehicle. You'll eventually be glad they're there.

• Don't carry your wallet in your pants pocket when checking water traps. If you're operating out of a vehicle, keep it in a secure place in the vehicle. If you're in a boat, put the wallet in a sealed plastic bag and put it in a dry well, toolbox, or similar safe place. You'll understand the

Keeping a trapline notebook will make you a better, more efficient trapper.

reason for this precaution on the same day you need the dry change of clothes.

• If you use a tile spade for your digging tool on a water trapline, trim a half-inch to an inch off each side of the blade. This allows you to dig smaller pockets for mink, and you can still dig larger holes almost as quickly and easily.

• Good trapline habits are as easy to form as bad ones. Don't lay your pliers on the ground when you've finished using them at a set; put them in your pocket instead, or you'll eventually leave them at a set. Don't lay your tile spade down; stick it upright in the mud near your set so it's more noticeable and you'll remember to take it with you when you leave.

• When water trapping in freezing conditions, set in moving water and on south-facing shorelines where possible. This keeps your traps working longer. Setting inside holes and under cut-banks also helps, as does choosing dark-soil locations for your sets. Even if you only gain an extra hour of open-water conditions each night, that may just be the hour your target animal comes through.

• Dry-land sets can be effectively freeze-proofed by sprinkling the bottom of the trap bed lightly with flaked calcium chloride (available at home supply warehouse stores and concrete manufacturing plants) or plain table salt, then adding more chloride or salt to your sifter and mixing that with the dirt as you cover and bed your trap. If land sets

A selection of digging tools for the trapline. The tile spade has ¾ inch trimmed off each side. The trowel is a homemade tool that is far sturdier than anything being commercially made, and the digging tool just below the sifter makes short work of digging a level-bottomed trap bed in dirt that's relatively free of rocks and roots.

are already made when cold weather is moving in, sprinkling chloride or salt on top of the dirt pattern will also work, but is not quite as effective. Make sure your traps are waxed before using this method of antifreezing, because both salt and calcium chloride are extremely corrosive.

• Invite a fellow trapper you like and trust to accompany you on your line, and ask him to make comments and criticisms as he watches you do your thing. I've done this many times and have never failed to pick up a tip or two, or a new way of looking at things.

• And, finally (you know this one's coming) . . . K.I.S.S.

Part II

MAKING YOUR SETS

9

Raccoon

My first raccoon was a grizzled old boar with a battle-scarred muzzle, notched ears, and toes missing from two feet. He was waiting for me at daylight, one hind foot in a number 2 longspring, in a trail set high on a pond bank.

There were so many things wrong with that set it's hard to know where to start. First, the trap was wrong. While a number 2 is acceptable for coons at a positive drowning set, it's a poor choice for high-and-dry locations because the larger jaw spread allows a coon to get under the jaws and chew on its foot.

Second, the set was in the wrong place. The trail led to the edge of the water, providing a perfect location where I could have drowned the coon easily.

Third, my fastening technique was awful. I'd wired the trap to a sturdy bush six feet from the set, using a single strand of rusty stovepipe wire. The wire was too long and too weak. If the coon hadn't wrapped about half the wire around the bush and the rest around both its foot and the trap, handcuffing itself and removing its ability to chew on its toes, I'd never have held it.

It worked out that time, but it shouldn't have. That set was no more appropriate for coons than for grizzly bears. My track record as a coon trapper up to that point—and for several years beyond—reflected my inexperience. I'd lost several coons before catching that grumpy old boar, and continued to lose most of my coon catches in the two or three seasons that followed. The reason was simple: I was doing it wrong. Coons are powerful animals, and their long, thin toes and tapered front foot, combined with that muscle power, make them hard to hold in foothold traps unless you do it right.

Eventually I figured it out: short chains, solid stakes, smaller traps, double jaws. All those things minimize the chance of a coon powering out or chewing out of your trap before you get there to collect him. Use adequate wire, too, if you're using wire to fasten coon traps. Nine-gauge is a little stiff for easy use, but 11-gauge is just about right. If you use 14-gauge, double it. If you use 16-gauge, stop.

TRAP STYLES AND SIZES
Coons have been caught in everything from number 0 weasel traps to number 5 beaver traps and from 110 to 330 body-grippers, but obviously some traps within this range are better than others.

Many veteran coon trappers swear by number 11 traps (the double longspring Number 1). This little trap is extremely strong, and its 4-inch jaw spread practically eliminates any foot damage from chewing. Other trappers like number 1 coilsprings for the same reasons.

The raccoon isn't a hard animal to get into a trap, but as many beginning trappers quickly learn, they can be hard to keep there.

*The best traps for coons are strong, compact, and have jaw spreads
small enough to keep trapped coons from getting underneath and
chewing on their feet. Top left: number 1 longspring guard-type trap.
Top right: number 11 longspring. Center left: number 1 coilspring. Center
right: number 1 double-jaw coilspring. Front: number 1½ coilspring.*

However, the small jaw spread of these traps often results in toe
catches and subsequent escapes, or outright misses. The larger jaw spread
of the 1½ coilspring reduces this problem, but introduces another: coons
can often get beneath the jaws to chew on their feet, causing excessive
foot damage and often escaping from the trap.

The guard-type traps used for shallow-water muskrat trapping are
also effective for coons, but since almost all guard traps are number 1
longsprings, the small jaw spread problem is in play. However, if you
have some guard traps in your inventory, they'll work for coons.

Double-jawed versions of the 11 longspring and 1½ coilspring help
reduce the chewing problem, but using drowning sets is the best solution.

DROWNING METHODS

The most effective thing a trapper can do to hold more coons in foothold
traps is to make drowning sets at every opportunity. Drowning is quick
and humane, results in fewer escapes, and practically eliminates foot
damage, regardless of the size of trap being used. Since most coons are
trapped near water, drowning is a practical option at many sets.

The surest and most humane way to hold coons after they're caught in foothold traps is to use high-percentage drowning sets.

Sometimes drowning isn't feasible, of course, such as on high-country predator lines where you'll catch big ridge-running boar coons. Those sets are covered later in this chapter. Usually, though, most coon trappers operate at the water's edge.

Slide-wire drowning rigs work well for all water-associated furbearers, as long as the water is deep enough to drown the target animal and as long as the trapper uses wires, stakes, weights, and traps that are big enough and sturdy enough. (Construction of slide-wire rigs is covered in chapter 8.)

Slide-wire rigs usually get the trapped animal away from the set location very quickly, keeping the animal from tearing up the set, and sliders also help reduce trapline theft. A live coon or other animal bouncing and squirming at the edge of the water can attract unwanted attention, but a drowned animal at the bottom of a slide wire is much less noticeable. Double-stake sliders are fine, provided the water is deep enough to drown the target animal and also shallow enough to wade and set the deep-end stake. If the water is too deep, though, or if the bottom is too hard to drive a stake, a drowning weight attached to the bottom end of the slide wire is better. A 15-pound rock, or 15 pounds of dirt or gravel in a mesh sack, is usually enough weight for coons and smaller animals. If beavers or otters are a possibility, double that amount of weight for best results.

Using a tangle stake is another method of drowning coons. In this method, drive the stake holding the trap into the bottom of the stream as far as possible from the bank, and then firmly drive a second stake (the tangle stake) into the bottom near the first one. The coon wraps the wire and chain around the tangle stake, is unable to return to the shore, and drowns. This method works okay, especially for mink and muskrats, but it's not as sure-fire for coons as the slide-wire drowner. I generally use it only when the water gets too deep to wade very close to the shore and I can't find suitable material for a weight on the deep-water end of a drowning rig.

Although most drowning sets are also water sets, that isn't a strict requirement. On occasion, I've run coons as far as 50 feet down a slider from the set location to get them into the water. The trick here is to make sure the wire or cable is tight as a bowstring and that there are no obstructions along the way to allow the coon to hang up. Having a fairly steep slope between the set location and the water doesn't hurt, either.

In cold weather, it's not absolutely necessary to drown a raccoon to ensure a fairly quick and humane end. If the water is eight inches deep or so, a coon unable to get back to the bank will succumb to hypothermia fairly quickly, and that depth of water is sufficient to keep it from gnawing on its trapped foot. Drowning is decidedly preferable to this technique, though, where the water is deep enough.

USE A HEAVY HAND
Raccoons are bold, curious, straight-ahead animals, and it pays to be pretty heavy-handed when trapping them. Using manmade eye appeal is one heavy-handed technique; for example, digging a large hole in the stream bank when making a pocket set, as discussed in the set-making section that follows.

Putting down a scent trail to your sets is another way to lay it on thick. It doesn't much matter what you use for the scent trail, so long as it's oily and smells of food. I save old bacon grease and cooking oil, adding juice from tuna, sardines, smoked oysters, and other canned meats as I use them. Then I add about 20 percent fish oil, pour the mixture into plastic squeeze bottles, and squirt a trail of this smelly juice from the top of the bank to my sets at the edge of the water.

FOOTHOLD SETS FOR RACCOONS

Throughout this discussion, remember that principle of heavy-handedness. If you'll give a raccoon something to investigate, he'll usually oblige.

Pocket sets are deadly for raccoons, but I like them big—a foot across, at least a foot high, and deep enough so the coon can't reach into the back of the pocket and fish out the bait without going over the trap. Twelve to fifteen inches deep is usually sufficient.

This is an extreme version of a big-hole pocket set. This abandoned beaver den entrance had washed out to an opening that was four feet wide. The trap stakes at each edge of the hole were left exposed to show the approximate location of the traps, which were set between the stakes and the vertical bank, with slide wires running to deep water in front of the hole. In a week's time, these two sets accounted for seven coons, three mink, and one muskrat.

Bed the trap in front of the hole, with the pan about four inches out from the pocket and about two to three inches left or right of center. The offset position allows for the width of the animal's body.

Bait is usually better than lure at a pocket set, because of the added visual appeal. However, make sure the bait isn't visible from above to prevent attracting raptors, crows, and other birds. I like a good-size bait—half a muskrat carcass, or a fist-size chunk of carp or other rough fish. It's a good idea to pin the bait to the back of the pocket with a sharp stick, in case the coon gets past the trap on the way in. If you make him work at getting the bait free, he'll eventually get caught.

The plastic pipe set is another highly effective coon set that relies on eye appeal. This one is effective everywhere there's a shoreline being used by coons, and it's fast and simple. Its only drawback is its visibility, which can lead to trap theft in some places.

This set's key element is a 12-inch section of white PVC pipe about two or three inches in diameter. Shove the section of pipe into the bank about six inches above the water's edge and shave a short section of the bank vertical right in front of the pipe. Bed your trap firmly in front of the pipe, in two to six inches of water and four to six inches out, and run the drowning wire to deeper water. Stuff a chunk of fish, muskrat, or your favorite raccoon lure into the pipe, squirt a scent trail from the high bank to the set, and you're done. Some longline coon trappers use this set almost exclusively to catch hundreds of coons every season.

Hollow logs and trees along the water's edge are raccoon magnets, but sometimes these are hard to set. Set them when it's convenient, but if there's not good place to bed the trap at the opening of a log or tree, simply use the log or tree as a visual attractor and make a pocket or PVC pipe set nearby. K.I.S.S., remember?

Trail sets are deadly for raccoons, but coon trails don't always enter the water at a convenient place to make a drowning set. Often, the water will be too shallow for a long way out from the set. Or, coons will enter the water to get around an obstruction, but the obstruction itself is a hindrance to an effective drowning set. Remember, you don't want anything near the set that will allow the coon to tangle up and not go down the wire.

On flat, featureless banks where coons' tracks are present but there are no well-defined trails, the old shiny-pan set is effective. This set has been described in trapping books for a hundred years, and it sounds too amateurish to work, but it's actually an excellent coon set where the water is clear. Simply cover the pan of the trap with aluminum foil and set the trap in the edge of the water, bedding it firmly with the pan two

Never pass up a log like this along a stream or lake bank. Note the coon laying on the log in the foreground; this illustrates the importance of setting more than one trap for coons, since they often travel in pairs or groups.

The amateurish-looking shiny pan set is deadly for coons when used properly, but it can lead to trap theft if used where human traffic is likely.

or three inches beneath the surface. Squirt a scent trail down the bank to the trap. If you've never tried this set, you'll be surprised how well it works—and it'll take a few mink as well.

Dirt-hole type sets, used primarily for canines and other upland predators, are effective for coons as well. Dirt-hole sets can be used effectively practically anywhere coons travel, but I use them mostly on high banks along streams, on sand bars, around abandoned farm buildings, and in other places where I know coons are traveling but can't find any well-defined trails.

There are many, many ways to make a dirt-hole set, and every one of those variations will catch coons, but here's the way I usually do it for coons: First, as with the pocket set, I dig a big hole if the dirt is soft enough, one that resembles something dug by a woodchuck or armadillo. I want a hole about eight inches wide and at least that deep, and at a

Here's one common variation of the dirt hole set. Bait or lure goes in the hole, a squirt of urine goes onto the backing, and the stake is driven underneath the trap. The ring shows a good pan position, about six inches from the hole and offset about two inches.

fairly steep angle—not quite vertical, but close. The trap is staked solidly on a short chain, and the pan is offset an inch or two left or right, about six inches from the lip of the hole. I bed the trap solidly, with dirt packed firmly around the trap so it won't move if the coon steps on the springs or jaws, and use the dirt from the hole to create an obvious, eye-catching dirt pattern in a fan shape out from the hole. I usually just squirt a good slug of fish oil into the bottom of the hole, but as a change-up I'll use a chunk of fish or muskrat for bait. If foxes or bobcats are possible incidental catches, I'll squirt a shot of red fox urine above the hole.

Several brands of specialized, raccoon-specific foothold traps have been developed for use where cats, dogs, and other undesirables are common—Egg Traps, Duffer Traps, Coon Cuffs, Bandit Busters, Li'l Griz Get'rz (really, that's the actual name). These traps all have one thing in common—the coon must stick its paw into a hole in the trap and fire the trap by moving the trigger. The traps are dog-proof, and almost cat-proof as well, and are pretty effective on coons. However, they're expensive, and some brands are hard to set.

BUCKETS FULL OF COONS
Where it's legal, and in locations where theft or domestic animals and pets aren't a problem, using body-grippers in plastic buckets or wooden boxes is extremely effective for coons. Both the 160 and 220 body-grippers, with jaw spreads of six and seven inches, are good.

Round buckets, square buckets, homemade wooden boxes, and other containers are all suitable. Cut slots in two sides of the container large enough to fit the springs of the trap (about two inches deep by ½ inch wide). Set the bucket where coons travel, throw some loud-smelling bait such as fish in the back of the bucket, set the trap in the bucket, cock the springs up or down slightly to lock the trap in place, and stake the trap in place or wire it to a nearby limb or root. If the bucket is tippy or unsteady, brace it with logs, rocks, or whatever is handy.

Using a few buckets to shortstop the coons at good upland predator set locations is often a good idea. Not only does it keep the coons out of the foothold sets, it also adds to the size of the fur check.

Many trappers camouflage buckets with dark spray paint, but I prefer to leave them white because of the increased degree of eye you-know-what. If I can see the bucket better, I figure the coon can, too. However, I do have a few camouflaged buckets for use where theft is a possibility.

SNARES AND BODY-GRIPPERS IN TRAILS
Snares are effective for coons, but where 160 or 220 sized body-grippers are legal for dry-land use, snares are rarely necessary. Because a snared coon usually has a lot of pelt damage, I rarely use snares for coons except for nuisance control work where pets are present.

Snares are very effective for upland predators when used in the right places, such as on this crossing log. With a loop diameter of six to seven inches and the bottom of the loop four inches high, snares will take coons, bobcats, foxes, and an occasional coyote. When targeting coyotes, a 10-inch loop 9 to 12 inches off the ground is a better option, but it will miss most of the other furbearers.

Snares are most effective on well-defined travelways, such as trails through thick weeds, on log crossings, and where coons are using beaver dams as bridges to cross streams. A loop size of six to seven inches is best, with the bottom of the loop about four inches high. Most snaremen use $5/64$ or $3/32$ cable for coons, but if the snare can be rigged as a drowning set $1/16$-inch cable is a good choice.

Body-grippers in the sizes mentioned above are very effective in the same types of travelways where snares are used, and they have the added advantages of killing the coon quickly and causing minimum disturbance to the set, and also making the captured animal less conspicuous. Body-grippers should never be used where pets might be caught.

CAGE TRAPS

Although wire cage traps are expensive and bulky, they have a place on many coon lines. Coons are attracted to the doings of humans—gardens, farm buildings, dumpsters behind fast-food joints, and so forth—and large catches can be made in these places. However, since pets and people are also present, conventional traps are seldom advisable.

Cage traps are the answer. If a dog or cat is caught, it's easy to release it unharmed, and using cage traps will get a trapper invited into places where he couldn't go with other types of traps.

Cages are used the same way buckets are used. Set the trap where coons are traveling, toss some attractive bait in the back of the trap, brace the trap with weights or stakes if it's unsteady, and come back later and get your coon. One thing I've found helpful is covering the cage with a piece of old blanket, carpet, or other material so that it forms a kind of tunnel. It seems that coons are more inclined to enter the trap when it's covered, and the covering also makes it much easier to handle a skunk, which you will have to do pretty often if you use cage traps much. Simply walk up to the covered trap from the side and pick it up, cover and all, and dispose of the skunk as described in chapter 20.

SET ENOUGH TRAPS

Raccoons often travel in groups, whether they're related or not. A female and her young may still be together when trapping season opens, and often two or more adult boar coons will pal around together. Even when coons travel by themselves, in good habitat, several of them may come by your set in a given night.

Therefore, the wise trapper uses more than one set at each location. Multiple catches aren't possible unless you have multiple sets. This is especially important when you're only going to be in an area a short

Because of their sensitive feet and their habit of feeling for their food, coons are apt to dig up poorly bedded traps and can sometimes become savvy to dirt-hole types sets. Bed your traps well and pack down all loose dirt, and you'll catch those coons the first time they visit. Presto, no trap-savvy coons.

while, because once a trap has made a catch, it's out of commission until you remove the catch and remake the set.

BEDDING

Bed all your traps firmly when you're after raccoons. In water sets, this can usually be accomplished by twisting the trap back and forth while applying downward pressure on it, squashing it into the mud. On dry land, if the soil is good, it's usually pretty easy to bed the trap firmly as well.

In rocky areas, both in and out of the water, it's often necessary to fiddle around with the bedding, sticking small rocks under the jaws and frame until the trap doesn't move when touched. This is aggravating sometimes, but do it. It's a very important step, because a raccoon makes much of its living by feeling around and finding things with its sensitive feet. If it steps on part of the trap and the trap moves, the almost inevitable result is that the coon will feel around underwater and find the trap (or dig into the dirt and find it, in the case of a dry set), then flip it over.

The coon doesn't do this because he's smart and knows it's a trap, but because he's curious and is looking under there to see if there's anything to eat. The bad thing is, the experience often teaches a raccoon to feel for traps in front of pockets and dirt-holes, and in that case he becomes a real trapline nuisance. Bed your traps solidly, and the first encounter the coon has with a trap will be its last, and he'll never have the chance to become trap-savvy.

There are hundreds of other ways to make effective coon sets, and the trapper is limited only by his own imagination. On a bet, I once caught a coon in a dirt-hole set using Chanel Number 5 perfume, and I caught one on another bet using a white glove as the only attractor. The key to effective raccoon trapping, as in all other types of trapping, is keeping things simple. Find a few sets that work for you in your area, and stick with them.

10

Muskrat

Muskrats are unwary and easily trapped, but many things can mean the difference between a so-so harvest and catching them in good numbers. Because of their abundance, coast-to-coast distribution, and ease of capture, muskrats are one of the most important and commonly sought furbearers, by beginning trappers and veterans alike. Most trappers will have access to at least some muskrat trapping, and the pelts usually have enough value to make them worthwhile targets.

Of course, some parts of the country have more muskrat potential than others. A trapper operating in the Nevada high desert won't need as many muskrat traps as a farmland trapper in central Illinois. But where there's suitable habitat, you'll probably find a few muskrats, even in unlikely places. I've seen muskrats in high, isolated ponds on ridgetops in the Appalachians, in stock ponds in the Wyoming sagebrush country, in clear, freestone Colorado trout streams with little streamside vegetation, and in the large, rocky, manmade lakes in the Ozarks.

The most productive muskrat habitats are usually freshwater or brackish marshes, both inland and along the coast. Populations in the more fertile marshes can be astounding, and trappers on the better marshes (such as those along the Atlantic Coast and Lake Erie and many of the prairie pothole marshes in the Upper Midwest) routinely catch from four to ten muskrats per acre. In peak population years, catch rates can be several times higher.

In recent years, though, the trend for marsh-dwelling muskrat populations has been sharply downward. There are still excellent marsh 'rat populations in some areas, but in many marshes where muskrats were once abundant, they are now practically extinct. Whether this is related to disease, pesticide buildup, or other factors has yet to be determined at this writing, but the trend is nationwide. In Louisiana, much of the muskrat decline has been blamed on competition from the nutria, a South American rodent imported to Louisiana in the 1930s.

While they rarely reach the high densities found in good marshes, muskrat populations in streams, lakes, and irrigation ditches haven't been hit with whatever it is that's reduced marsh muskrat populations. Probably more muskrats have been taken in recent years in stream, lake, and ditch type habitats than in marshes.

TRAP SIZES AND STYLES

Like raccoons, muskrats are easier to get into a trap than they are to keep there. Muskrats aren't strong animals, and they can't power out of a trap or chew their feet like coons, but their front legs are delicate and the bones break easily. Many thousands of muskrats are lost each year because the 'rat wrings its front foot off and escapes. Often the muskrat dies after the experience, but not always. I've caught many fat, healthy, three-legged muskrats whose missing limb had healed, and I've even caught a few who were missing both front feet and were still apparently healthy and getting along fine.

But, of course, the object of trapping muskrats isn't to collect their feet. The best way to avoid this problem is to use body-grippers so muskrats are killed quickly when they hit the trap, or to drown the muskrat quickly when using foothold traps so they can't wring off a foot and escape.

The muskrat is the most commonly caught furbearer for most trappers and represents a good portion of the nation's fur sales.

Good muskrat traps include: top row, left to right—number 2 long-spring, number 1 longspring, number 1 longspring Victor guard trap; second row—number 11 longspring, number 1 longspring Blake & Lamb guard trap; third row—number 2 coilspring, number 1 ¾ coilspring; front—number 1 ½ coilspring. All these traps are small but heavy and will quickly drown a trapped muskrat if the set is made so the animal can reach a foot or more of water.

The 110 body-gripper probably accounts for more muskrats than all other traps combined, and I use them a lot. I also use a good many 160s for muskrats, especially in underwater sets. But many good muskrat sets just don't lend themselves to body-grippers, and my personal list of suitable footholds for muskrats is long and varied. I use more 1½ coilsprings than anything else, but that's because I have more of them. Other perfectly fine 'rat traps include 1, 1½, and 2 longsprings and 1, 1¾, and 2 coilsprings. Guard-type traps are also useful at shallow-water sets where there's not enough water to drown a muskrat and where body-gripper traps won't work well, such as feed beds in very shallow water.

SETS FOR MUSKRATS

Muskrats are territorial and, except for the spring breeding season, spend most of their lives in a very small area. In still-water habitats like marshes and ponds, they leave an abundance of sign—droppings, slides, houses, feed beds, aquatic vegetation cuttings floating on the surface—but in streams there may be little or no muskrat sign even where 'rats are fairly plentiful.

"Setting on sign" is the best option. It's hard to beat a feed bed set, and it's very simple to make. A feed bed is a semi-floating nest-like collection of cuttings made where muskrats sit while they eat their food, usually roots, grasses, and underwater vegetation. The uneaten portions of these plants are discarded on the spot, and eventually a feed bed forms. These are usually in fairly shallow water, but can also be in deep water where a 'rat sits on a slightly submerged or barely exposed limb or stump. Muskrats also like to make feed beds under overhanging pond or stream banks, where they have overhead protection from hawks and owls.

Muskrat tracks on a muddy bank. Note the drag mark made by the 'rat's tail.

All that's necessary to catch a 'rat at a feed bed is to wiggle a foothold trap into the center of the bed, pushing it down far enough into the mat of vegetation so the trap is covered with water. If the mat is too dry, too buoyant, or too solid to get the trap underwater, simply remove some of the material from the feed bed or cover the trap very lightly with cuttings from the bed. Attach an extension wire to the trap chain so that wire and chain total about two feet, and wire the trap to a stake stuck into the bottom. If the water is less than a foot deep, use a guard trap; otherwise, any of the traps mentioned previously will work fine.

Muskrat toilets also make excellent set locations, but sometimes they're hard to set. Muskrats leave their small, oblong droppings on logs, rocks, and streamside structure such as small points and peninsulas, and several muskrats may use the same toilet. Simply set a foothold trap in the water in front of the droppings and stake it in deeper water as noted above.

Muskrats create runs (sometimes called slides) when they leave streams or ponds and go up into adjacent fields or cross into adjacent waterways, and these are excellent set locations for both foothold and body-gripper traps. If I'm using footholds, I prefer setting at the edge of the water so I can drown the catch, but with body-grippers, the best set location is usually at the top of the bank where the slide hits level ground, or at a point along the slide where it passes through grass, brush, or other vegetation where it's easier to break up the trap's outline. You can also create very effective sets by using a booted foot or your gloved hand to make artificial runways, slicking up the bank and making it look like muskrats have been going up the slope there. Set the traps as described above.

Excellent set locations are at muskrat den entrances in ditch banks, pod dams, and other places where shorelines are steep enough and firm enough to support a tunnel. In clear, still water, these can often be found by sight, by looking for the plume of muddy water made by 'rats as they enter and leave the tunnel. Simply place a 110 or 160 body-gripper (depending on the size of the hole) in the mouth of the den, brace it in place with a stick through the springs, and wire it to a stake or streamside bush. Sometimes it's possible to take a dozen muskrats from a single den entrance, but three or four is more the norm.

Muskrat houses also make excellent set locations for muskrats (for mink, too, provided the house is within 15 feet or so of dry land). The entrance to the muskrat house will always be underwater, and there will often be two or more entrances, but these can be hard to find and harder to set because of the ragged underwater construction of most muskrat

Setting muskrat houses is illegal in some states, but where legal, it's very effective.

houses. The best option, in my opinion, is to find the landing spot on the muskrat house and set it instead.

There's almost always a landing spot, and it's usually pretty obvious. The typical 'rat house has a steep side and a gently sloping side, and muskrats often climb onto the sloping side to preen, loaf, and do whatever else it is that muskrats do when they come out of the water. They occasionally use these flat places for feed beds or toilets, but it's been my experience that this is unusual and they usually go elsewhere for eating and excreting. Simply bed a foothold trap in the edge of the water on the gently sloping side of the house, and wire it away from the house so the 'rat will hit the water and drown. Sometimes the loafing area will be big enough for two sets, and doubles are common. Set the traps at least a foot apart and run the chains and wires in opposite directions to minimize the chance of a muskrat getting caught in both traps.

Underwater swim channels and runways are common in good muskrat territory. These little fellows swim on the surface in deep water but do much of their shallow-water traveling along the bottom. In doing so, they wear well-defined grooves in the bottom. Sometimes you can see these, and sometimes you can find them with your feet. However you find them, set them. Use 110 or 160 body-grippers, and place from one to three or four traps at five- to ten-foot intervals in the runway, bracing them in place with stabilizers or sticks through the springs. Multiple catches are common.

These underwater channels can also be set effectively by using colony-type traps. These are wire cages, either homemade or commercially made, that allow rats to enter but not leave. Some of them operate on the trap-door principle, so that the 'rat pushes the door up and passes into the trap, but then the trap door falls back into place and prevents escape. Other cage traps have a funnel entrance at one or both ends, with a small (4-inch) hole through which the muskrats pass going in. They can't find the small hole in time to escape, and drown. I've caught as many as five muskrats in a single check in cage traps on hot runways.

The bottom edge set is deadly for muskrats along small streams. Just look at the stream's outside shoreline, the one that catches most of the current flow, and find a bump, rock, clump of grass roots, or anything else that sticks out farther into the current than the rest of the bank. Set a 110 or 160 body-gripper tight against the shoreline obstruction and flush against the stream bottom, in six inches to two feet of water. Brace the trap in position with a stick through the jaws, and you're through. This set also takes good numbers of mink, which is why it's described in detail in the mink chapter.

You may have noticed that all the muskrat sets described so far have been blind sets or sets that do not rely on bait or lure. That's largely because of the K.I.S.S. rule. In most cases, you can make good muskrat catches without using either, and if you don't need it, why use it?

But bait and lure are useful at some muskrat sets. One example is the float set, which is often the muskrat set I resort to on deep, fast streams where muskrats are present but natural set locations are scarce. A muskrat float is simply a few pieces of scrap lumber and logs, nailed together to form a floating V-shaped platform with a flat place to set a trap at the opening of the V. Use a heavy foothold trap (such as a 1½ or 2 longspring or a 2 coilspring), attached to the float with a two-foot length of wire. A longer wire is used to fasten the trap to a limb, log, anchor, or other secure object to keep the float where you want it. Put a wad of moss, leaves, or wadded-up grass into the back of the V, sprinkle a few drops of a good muskrat lure on the vegetation or on top of one of the logs forming the V, and set the trap on the platform between the logs. Hot locations for float sets include the slack-water eddies often found below rock piles or log drifts, brushy shorelines where it's difficult to reach the bank to make other types of sets, and bare, featureless shorelines on streams or ponds where there are no eye appeal locations.

One other effective set for those featureless banks is the simple bait set. Kick a slight indention into the shoreline with your boot, and at the

Muskrat Float—top view

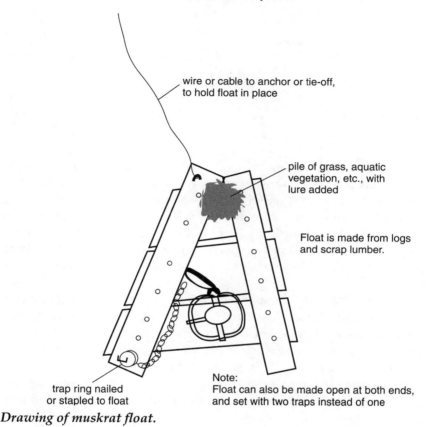

wire or cable to anchor or tie-off, to hold float in place

pile of grass, aquatic vegetation, etc., with lure added

Float is made from logs and scrap lumber.

trap ring nailed or stapled to float

Note:
Float can also be made open at both ends, and set with two traps instead of one

Drawing of muskrat float.

back of the indention, impale a slice of apple, pear, carrot, turnip, or parsnip on a stick and jab the stick into the mud. Set a foothold trap in the edge of the water at the indention and stake it in deeper water.

DON'T OVERSTAY YOUR WELCOME

Muskrat trapping is a game of quick returns or no returns. If you don't start catching them in good numbers the first night, you're either doing something wrong or the 'rats aren't there. The most effective and economical way of trapping muskrats is to hit an area pretty heavily for two or three days, then pull the sets and moving to another area. You can continue to catch the occasional 'rat in old sets, but it's neither cost-effective or labor-effective to keep the same sets out more than a week, and usually half that time is plenty if you've set it heavily enough.

The main things to remember in muskrat trapping are to hit 'em hard, get 'em quick, and move on down the road. And, of course, K.I.S.S.

11

Mink

Compared to raccoons and muskrats, mink are relatively scarce. Even where mink populations are high, you'll never find them in densities like muskrats or raccoons, even in the best habitat. They're solitary animals and avoid one another except during the late-winter mating period and when a female is raising her young during the summer. More than one mink will occupy the same territory, but they never travel together. Mink are secretive and seldom seen, and in most cases they don't leave a lot of sign.

All these things combine to create the false impression that mink are smart and hard to catch. Catching a mink may be more difficult than catching a muskrat in the sense that muskrats are more plentiful, but the average mink is no more wary or trap-savvy than the average muskrat. They're not hard to catch; they're hard to find.

Many trappers erroneously believe a mink is a water animal. Instead, a mink is a water-associated animal. Put another way, a mink is a land animal that often enters the water. It's not uncommon for individual mink, particularly adult males, to spend days or weeks away from water, catching birds and mice in fields and brushy areas. Upland trappers occasionally catch mink in fox, coyote, and bobcat sets far from water.

Of course, that's not the way to make good mink catches. Most mink do the majority of their hunting and traveling along the shorelines of creeks, rivers, ponds, and lakes, and it's at this interface between the dry and the wet where you're going to catch them.

If you want to catch mink in large numbers, there's really only one option: cover a lot of ground. Remember, there aren't many mink in a given area, and if you want to catch many of them, you'll have to go to them.

The average mink has a bigger home range than the average raccoon or muskrat. If your sets are much less than a mile apart, chances are you're setting for the same mink at both locations. In most cases, you'll catch more mink by spacing your set locations farther apart and spreading them out over a larger territory than by crowding your locations together.

When you do set up a location for mink, it's always a good idea to make more than one set there. Mink don't travel together, but several mink are probably passing through the area. A single good set at each stop on your line will catch a lot of mink, but you'll miss a lot of them, too. In good mink habitat, it's a good idea to make two, three, four, or even more sets at most of the stops on your line. A single trap gives you only one shot at catching a mink, and if anything happens, you're shot. A water level rise, a freeze, a shift in wind direction at a lured or baited set, or any number of things can happen to effectively put you out of commission at a single-set stop. Or the mink might run the other side of the creek. Even if your single trap connects with a muskrat or coon (or even another mink), you're out of business at that location until you run and reset your traps.

However, don't go overboard. At practically any good mink location in my territory or yours, there are many places that would make good mink sets. It's easy to go into overkill mode, especially if the location has a lot of potential set structure in the form of cut banks, spring runs, feeders, hollow logs, brush piles, crossing logs, and the like. I rarely set fewer than two or more than five traps at a single stop on my line.

The mink, contrary to what most trappers think, is not a water animal.

Mink aren't hard to catch, but they don't occur in large concentrations in most areas, so a trapper must cover a lot of ground to catch them in good numbers.

The exceptions are when I only have a short time to trap a given location, or when I see sign of an exceptionally high population of incidental furbearers such as coons or muskrats. In these cases, I may go ahead and make a dozen or so sets. In the first case, I'm trying to maximize my chance of connecting with every mink that comes through during my limited time at that location. In the second, I'm trying to knock back the population of other furbearers as quickly as possible, after which I thin the traps back to three or four of the best sets.

Cover as many travel routes with your sets as possible. A mink has erratic travel patterns, not only regarding its movements over its home range, but also in the specific travel routes it uses as it comes through the place where you've set your traps. On one trip under a bridge, a mink may be at the water's edge on the west side of the stream. When he

Mink leave relatively little sign in most situations. Places with this many mink tracks are rare.

comes back under the same bridge three days or three weeks later, he may be high on the east bank, 50 feet from the water. Or, he may go up the road embankment and cross the road. You just never can tell with a mink, which is why you need more than one set.

Few trapline situations are ideal, but ideally, here's how I like to set up a stop on my line: First, I look for water's edge sets, and I try to put at least one set on each side of the stream unless there's something that makes it clear all the water's edge mink traffic is on one side or the other. A steep bluff on one side of the stream is a good example. I use both leg-holds and body-grippers at these water's edge sets, depending on the situation.

Next, I move up on the high bank and look for a good trail set on each side, where I generally set a 110 body-gripper. I'll also set a body-gripper in any trail I find going up over the roadway. (Most of my mink sets are at bridges and culverts along roads.) This four-to-six-trap setup gives me a chance at every mink that comes along, regardless of its travel path on this particular trip through. If there are any obvious travelways between the high and low trails, I may set them as well, but these key locations produce the vast majority of my fur.

Many trappers use baited or lured pocket sets almost exclusively for mink trapping, but once you learn what to look for, I believe you can catch more mink in blind sets than in baited and lured sets. First, blind sets are quicker, and conform to the K.I.S.S. principle. Second, blind sets aren't as likely to attract coons, possums, skunks, or muskrats. Third, a mink reacting to lure or bait will be on the alert and not acting naturally, and I believe it's a lot easier to get a mink to step on or pass through a trap when it's acting naturally and is not alerted.

That's not gospel, certainly, and I do use quite a few lured sets and even a few baited sets, especially late in the season. But I still think most mink trappers overdo it with bait and lure and would catch more mink if they used more blind sets.

Stay with it and don't get discouraged. This is the most important thing if you're going to catch many mink. If you want to catch them in numbers, there's only one way: set a lot of traps, and run them for a lot of days. Mink trapping, even under the best of conditions, is not a high-percentage game. My records show I average about 1.8 mink per 100 trap nights—and my trapline is in excellent mink country. Some days I do much better than that, but there are also times when I do much worse.

Also, keep an open mind. Nothing in mink trapping is 100 percent. I use mostly blind sets, but I use bait and lure too. I use 110s in most dry sets, but I also use some legholds and even a few snares. There will

The pocket set in its many variations is the only set used by many mink trappers. This is a mistake. Using a combination of blind sets, pocket sets, high-bank sets, and other effective mink sets described in this chapter is the way to run an efficient mink line.

always be exceptions to the rule. And don't take everything you read in this book as gospel, either, regarding mink trapping or anything else.

Experiment. If you see an unusual situation on your line, or if you think of an oddball trick that just might work in this situation or that one, by all means, try it. I've caught many mink and other furbearers in once-in-a-lifetime situations, and I expect to catch many more in the future. All that's required is that you recognize these opportunities when they arise and figure out how to take advantage of them.

TRAP SIZES AND STYLES

Mink are more forgiving than most furbearers regarding trap sizes. I don't know that I've ever caught a mink in a number 0 trap, but that's because I've almost never used them. However, I'm sure the 0 would hold mink.

This is why the 1½ coilspring is the author's favorite mink trap. It gets a high grip on the mink's leg, is heavy enough to drown the mink quickly, and virtually eliminates escapes when tuned and set properly.

Two traps serve in more than 90 percent of my mink trapping—the 1½ coilspring and the 110 body-gripper. But I don't like them the way they come out of the box, and I modify them as described in chapter 3. The crisp let-off and stronger springs in the 1½ and the looped trigger on the 110 make both much more efficient for mink.

However, many good mink trappers favor other styles, particularly the number 11 longspring. I have no quarrel with these trappers, but I personally feel the 1½ coilspring outperforms the 11 because it's faster and has a larger jaw spread, both of which let it get a higher grip on the mink's leg.

Other traps that sometimes find their way onto my mink line are the number 2 longspring, the 1.75 coilspring, and the 160 body-gripper. I use the larger footholds when I want a heavier trap to pull my catch down quickly to get it out of sight. I use the 160s at many underwater swim-through sets, such as the bottom edge set described below, because the larger jaw area makes for a bigger passageway mink to swim through. A mink will often slip through and avoid the triggers of a 160 in a dry set, but underwater they'll almost always fire the trap.

SETS FOR MINK

Whether it's a small tile draining a field or a huge, corrugated thing you can walk through under a road, pipes and culverts are mink magnets. Often, a blind set at the edge of the water, with the trap placed tight against the culvert in the very edge of the water, is all that's needed. Almost every mink that comes through will slide along the bank and slip into the end of the culvert. The best set locations are usually, but not always, on the downstream side. On larger culverts, set both sides and both upstream and downstream if possible. In most cases, footholds are the best choice here, but body-grippers can be used in some locations. As with the set descriptions below, use your own judgement and use which-ever trap you think is the best choice.

Natural pockets are naturals. Any hole along a stream, especially one that has an entrance at the water's edge, is a hot mink set location. At smaller holes, put the trap in the center of the hole and right at its mouth. However, some natural pockets are too large to guard with a trap set in the middle of the hole. In this case, crowd the trap against one side of the hole or the other, or use two traps and set both sides. When the mink explores a larger hole, it will slip around the side of the hole rather

Pipes and culverts at the water's edge are mink magnets. Never pass one up without examining it closely for set-making opportunities.

than centering it, the way a coon will do. I prefer to use no bait or lure at natural pockets and let the hole itself serve as the attractor.

As we've already mentioned, many mink trappers rely almost exclusively on baited and lured artificial pocket sets, and they catch a lot of mink. The obvious advantage of using artificial pockets is that the trapper can put the pocket where he wants it, without having to go looking for a natural hole that may or may not be convenient to set and check.

There are dozens of ways to dig pockets, and no doubt you'll develop your own preferences, but the advice from this corner is to not overthink this issue. In my opinion, the best hole is the K.I.S.S. hole. I use a tile spade to punch a four-inch-wide hole a foot or so straight back into a relatively steep bank at the water's edge, and set a trap under about a half-inch of water in the mouth of the pocket. Add bait or lure if you wish, but I set at least half of my artificial pockets without either bait or lure, and I've never been able to detect a difference in the success rates.

Where a stream has washed out the dirt beneath streamside vegetation, there will usually be an overhang that provides several things for a mink: a convenient travelway, overhead cover from avian predators, and a productive place to search for food. Leghold or body-gripper traps set under these overhangs are almost surefire mink-getters.

Along stream banks, particularly at outside bends, you'll often find piles of leaves, sticks, grass, and other debris washed up in piles by floodwaters. These drifts often form a barricade to mink traveling along the stream, but you can turn these piles into mink funnels by simply kicking a hole through the drift (or ramming a stout stick through) near the water's edge and guarding the hole with a body-gripper or leghold. These are extremely fast, effective sets, and you should never pass up the opportunity to make one.

The bottom edge set, popularized and perfected by Michigan trapper Ken Smythe around 1990, is a natural blind set that catches large numbers of muskrats, but it will also nail many mink if made in the right place. The key features to look for are slight bumps in the shoreline that stick out into a stream on the deep-water side of the flow, such as a clump of grass, a root system, or a rock. The set can be made in four or more feet of water, but it's most effective—and easier to make—when the water depth is from six inches to two feet. It's simple in the extreme: position a 110 or 160 body-gripper tight against the shoreline bump and flush against the bottom, brace it in place with a stick shoved through the spring into the bottom, and wire the trap to something above water. This set is best when cold weather arrives, but it will produce mink all season long.

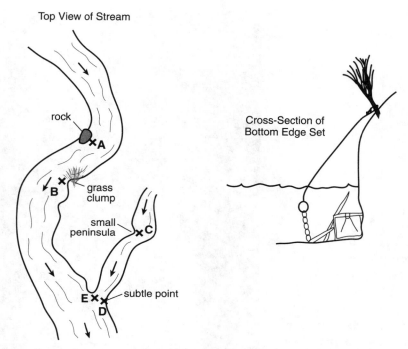

Top View of Stream

rock

×A

B×

grass
clump

small
peninsula

×C

E××
D

subtle point

Cross-Section of
Bottom Edge Set

*Locations for the bottom edge set: A—anywhere a rock, log, tree, or
other obstruction creates a bump sticking out from the rest of the bank
is a top location for this set. B—grass clumps often form humps in otherwise straight banks and make good bottom edge locations. C—small
peninsulas of dirt or gravel sometimes form on the inside bends of
creeks, and where the water is deep enough (five to six inches), make
good bottom edge locations. D—sometimes the bank bumps are very
subtle, such as at the confluence of two streams, but the location is still
a top choice for the bottom edge set. E—the point of land at the Y of
two small streams, or a small stream with a larger one, can be a prime
location if the current is swift enough to keep a sand bar from forming
at the V. If the water is deep enough at the point to cover a body-gripper
trap, set it.*

Logs across streams are used as bridges by mink, and they can be
easily and effectively set using body-grippers. The easiest way to brace
the trap in place is by driving three or four small nails (I prefer four, for
extra stability) into the log, spacing them so that the trap's jaws firmly
grip the nails and hold it in place. This requires a little experimentation
at each set to get the spacing right, but it takes only a second. Any size
log is good; just make sure your trap is set on the crown of the log's

Set mink body-grippers on the crown of the crossing log, regardless of the size of the log. This log was plenty big enough for mink to avoid the trap if they wanted to, but this set produced more than a dozen mink in three trapping season before a flood washed the log away.

curve, because that's where the mink will run. You can catch mink with a bare trap set like this, but it's better to drape a stick or twig over the jaws, so the mink will duck and go through the trap rather than jumping over it.

The elbow pocket set is the most complicated mink set I use on my line, and therefore I don't use it very often. It is constructed by digging a standard pocket, then going up on the bank above the pocket and digging nearly straight down to connect with it, forming an elbow-shaped tunnel with two entrances—one at water level and one on the higher bank. I use elbows when I can't decide whether the mink are running the high bank or the water's edge, or where the water level of a stream fluctuates too much for a standard pocket set to remain effective. I usually use a body-gripper set at the lower hole, and sometimes a foothold bedded in the entrance of the upper hole.

Water levels fluctuate in both ponds and streams, and it only takes an inch or two either way to put most mink sets out of commission. The elbow pocket helps some in this regard, but only if the water level stays below the upper entrance. The wise trapper hedges his bets by setting body-grippers in high-bank trails along waterways. These high sets catch mink even in dry weather, because a certain percentage of mink will run the high bank when they're not actively searching for food. But when these sets really shine is when a rain causes a substantial rise in water level. Your traditional water's edge sets will be out of commission, but those high-bank sets in rabbit trails and at natural pinch points farther up the bank will keep you skinning mink.

LOCATION, LOCATION, LOCATION

As you can see from the above section, most effective mink sets are pretty simple. However, they must be made in the right spots before they can be effective. Locating the likely mink travelways is the key.

Some travelways are obvious. Some are not. The illustration shows a composite of typical mink habitat and the most likely travelways. Some of these were discussed in the set-making section above. Not every place on your line will have all these types of locations, of course, but that's

Locations For Mink Sets

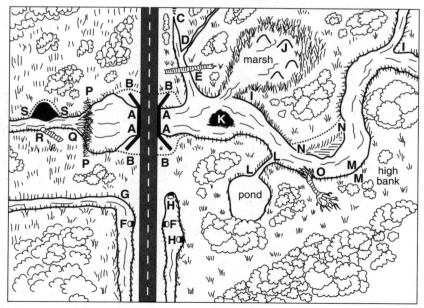

Likely mink set locations.

okay—it just decreases the decision making you have to do at a particular stop. Remember, you don't need a trap at every good-looking place. Two to four sets at each stop is my usual work plan.

A. At the intersection of every waterway with a road, there will be a bridge, metal culvert, concrete box culvert, or some other passageway for the water to get underneath the road. This is the number one, primo place for sets, since traveling mink are forced into a narrower pathway because of the constriction of the bridge and because these are the easiest and quickest locations to check. Every bridge is different, though, and you need to size each one up and set it accordingly, using blind leghold sets, blind body-gripper sets, pockets, cubbies, or whatever. If the water is flowing swiftly through the culvert, the best set locations are generally on the downstream side. At some bridges and culverts, the best sets will be underneath the roadway itself.

B. Don't overlook the possibility that mink are traveling up and over the road rather than through the bridge or culvert. Many mink, especially big boars, do this. Look for dim trails through the grass of the road embankment going up and over the road, and guard them with body-grippers. You'll catch rabbits, skunks, and possums, but you'll catch a lot of mink as well.

C. If there's a drainage ditch or canal along the roadway where you're traveling, where it heads up is a fine location for mink sets. The water is usually shallower here, and mink almost always follow these waterways to their end.

D. Any small feeders coming off canals or small waterways should also be given consideration for sets. The point of land is sometimes the best set location, but if the feeder is small and shallow enough, a trap right in the mouth of the feeder will often produce.

E. Logs spanning waterways are hot set locations, for mink and almost every other furbearer as well. You might find good sets at each end of the log, on the middle of the log itself, or beneath the log on either side of the stream or ditch. If no logs are there naturally, you can place small ones at strategic locations. Even old boards will work if logs aren't available.

F. Mink are likely to cross the road anywhere there are non-connecting water bodies such as ditches, ponds, or canals on both sides of the road. Sometimes there will be a culvert under the road at these points, and if that's the case, check carefully at both ends for signs of mink passage. If there's no culvert (or even if there is), check the grassy road embankment for signs of a trail through the grass, like the ones that can often be found at A.

G. Where a manmade drainage or irrigation ditch makes a sharp turn and heads off in a new direction is sometimes a hotspot, and you might find good locations on both sides of the waterway at this point.

H. Where a well or drainage pipe empties its discharge into a waterway is a red-hot mink set location. If these pipes are at water level, sets can be made directly in the end of the pipe. If they're above water level (which is usually the case), sets can be made underneath or near the pipe at waterline.

I. Anywhere two bodies of water intersect, there's almost sure to be mink activity. Check these places closely, and set them accordingly.

J. Muskrat houses can make effective mink sets. However, your odds for success will be higher if you target the houses closest to the shoreline. Mink don't hesitate to swim, but don't forget that they're basically land animals.

K. Likewise, beaver houses can sometimes make good mink set locations. However, the large sticks and logs used in most beaver houses sometimes make picking a good set location tricky. It might be best to make mink sets along the shoreline near the house rather than on the house itself.

L. Small trickles that drain ponds or lakes into streams are good set locations, whether they're dry or full of water. The hottest set locations along these small drains are usually, but not always, at the ends.

M. High banks along the outside bend of waterways are good locations for a high-low approach. Some mink will run the waterline, while others stick to the top of the bluff. Check both places. In unstable water conditions, the high-bank sets will often save the day.

N. Also check out the inside bends of streams. There are usually sand, gravel, or mud bars at these places, and sets made at either end of the bars are good bets. Also, if the bend in the stream is sharp enough, many mink will take a shortcut overland across the peninsula.

O. Large fallen trees or drift piles along waterways are also mink magnets, because mink know they are not only good places to find something to eat, but also safe places to hole up and eat what they catch. These places provide opportunities for a wide variety of sets—pockets, blind sets, high-bank sets, and others.

P. Beaver dams, like logs that have fallen across streams, are deadly places to catch mink and other furbearers. You can set on the dam itself or make pockets or other types of sets at either end. Be cautious here, though. On active dams, beavers will sometimes either cover your set with fresh layers of mud and debris or stick a toe into your set and get away with your trap.

Q. The trickles of water that come through beaver dams are also promising mink set locations. Sometimes you'll find the best sets right up against the dam, and sometimes they'll be several yards downstream.

R. Hollow logs, no matter where you find them along a stream, are good bets as well. If the log is small enough, it's often a good idea to put at least one end of it into the edge of the water to make an inviting place for a mink to investigate and an easy place to make a set.

S. Any obstruction that forces bank-running mink to either take to the water or climb the bank and go around is a high percentage set location. I usually set these up with high-low sets, similar to high bank set locations, to cover both possible travelways.

12

Otter

Otters have always been a desirable catch, but in recent years Asian demand has pushed prices dramatically upward. It's not surprising that trapping pressure on this sleek animal has increased sharply. Biologists have been monitoring otter populations, but thus far the increased pressure seems to have had little effect on otter numbers, and in fact otters are increasing and expanding their range in most parts of the country.

If you've ever had the chance to observe an otter in the wild for any length of time, you know why some trappers refer to otters as "creek rockets." Otters are as fast and nimble as seals, and make their living in the same way—by chasing down wild, healthy fish. This habit often makes them unpopular with fish farmers and fishermen. While it's true that otters sometimes cause serious depredation problems for fish farmers, research has shown that otters feed mostly on carp, suckers, and other rough fish rather than the bass, crappies, walleyes, and other game-fish anglers are most interested in. In many areas, otters also feed heavily on crawfish. They also on rare occasions eat snakes, turtles, and even muskrats.

But whatever an otter decides to dine on, you can bet your last steel trap he catches it in the water. In chapter 12, the mink was described as "a land animal that often enters the water." Reverse that and you have the otter—a water animal that often comes to land. The photo on page 124 shows one of my trapping partners with an otter he caught in a coyote set halfway up a mountain, more than a quarter-mile from the nearest water, but if you're trapping for otters, this isn't the way to bet. The hotspots for otter sets, almost always, are in the water or very near to it.

Unlike other water-based furbearers such as raccoons, muskrats, beavers, and even mink, otters are relatively scarce on a critters-per-square-mile basis, even in excellent habitat. The home ranges of several otter families may overlap, but over most of their range, otter populations run pretty thin.

In recent years, due to demand by the Chinese market, the otter has become the star of North American furbearers.

All by itself, this presents the otter trapper with a challenge. Compounding the problem are two more aggravating otter characteristics. First, otters travel extensively, and it may take them a week or more to come to your sets. Sometimes they'll remain in an area for several days if the hunting is good, but their usual habit is to hunt on the fly, rarely stopping anywhere for very long.

The second habit that makes otters more challenging than many other furbearers is their unpredictable nature. Otters often vary their route as they make their nearly ceaseless circles and loops through their home range. Fluctuating water levels, fish movements, and just plain otter unpredictability often cause them to come through an area on a different pathway than the last time through.

Aside from those factors, otters aren't particularly hard to catch. However, like beavers and raccoons, they can be very hard to hold if you don't use enough trap.

TRAP SIZES AND STYLES

Pound for pound, there's probably no more powerful furbearer than a big male otter. That means trappers must use strong, well-maintained equipment and fasten it well. You can catch otters in 11s and 1½s; I've done it. However, those catches were accidental, and I've lost far more otters in those traps than I've held.

The eight-inch jaw spread of the 280 body-gripper is ideal for otter trapping.

My favorite leghold trap for otter is the number 1.75 coilspring with number 3 springs and offset jaws. The 5 ⅜-inch jaw spread of this trap practically eliminates toe catches, and toe catches are the number one reason for otter pull-outs. Other good foothold otter traps are number 3, 4, and 5 longsprings and number 3, MB 650, and MB 750 coilsprings.

My favorite otter body-gripper is the 280, but the 220 is also good. The 330 is a serviceable otter trap, but its larger jaw spread allows some otters to pass through without firing the trap and others to get caught far back on the hips, resulting sometimes in pull-outs and other times in live otters in your traps. Neither of these outcomes is desirable. Regardless of the size body-gripper, research studies indicate that the best trigger position for catching otters is the standard V, with triggers on the bottom and positioned midway on the jaw, angled 45 degrees off center.

For snares, 3/32 cable is best for most situations. Snares made of 5/64 cable are more flexible and close more smoothly, but this size cable isn't heavy enough for otter unless you make surefire drowning sets. A six-inch loop size, just big enough to accommodate a grown man's fist, is about right for otters, with the bottom of the loop barely off the ground.

LAYING OUT AN OTTER LINE
One of the sad truths of trapping almost any furbearer in good numbers is that you have to cover a lot of territory to get the job done. This is especially true with nomadic, large-home-range critters like otters. If your aim is to get into double digits with your otter catch, you're probably going to have to put some miles on your vehicle.

Time is money, and these days, so is gasoline. In order to make your otter line as productive as possible you need a travel plan. Sit down with maps of your trapping area and mark the waterways. These are the otter travel routes. Then, try to "connect the dots" of these waterways by road so you can lay out your own travel route to cover as many of the otter travelways as possible.

It's hard to avoid backtracking with an auto line, for otters or anything else. Many of the best locations seem to be at the end of dead-end roads. Given current otter prices, it's sometimes worth it to go into these locations, since one otter can buy a lot of gas. But even with high-dollar fur, at some point backtracking becomes more time-consuming and expensive than it's worth. Could you tend more traps on down the line for the same or less mileage by ignoring that remote set location that's well off your main route? Is the side trip a hot enough location to justify the time and mileage? These are tough questions to answer, but the success of your otter line depends on them.

As with any other type of trapping, efficient otter trapping boils down to making the wisest use of your trapline time. Plan your line to hit as many likely otter locations as you can, and if this means omitting a few good places that are too far off your travel route, then so be it.

LOCATIONS AND SETS FOR OTTERS

The illustration on page 125 of a typical river system shows several high-percentage otter set locations. Those locations marked "A" are the upper and lower ends of sand bars or mud bars. These bars are usually on inside bends of streams where current is slower, and they're popular otter loafing and toilet areas. The downstream end is generally the

This otter was taken in a predator set several hundred yards from the nearest stream course, but that's not the type of place to make otter sets. Otters are creatures of the water, and almost all high-percentage otter sets will be either under water or within a very few feet of the water's edge.

highest-percentage location, but don't neglect the upstream end. It may well be the hotspot.

If otters are using a bar, you'll find evidence—tracks, droppings, scuffed-up sand or mud where they've played and rolled, balled-up mud, and debris. Sometimes you can narrow the approach enough to use a body-gripper or snare, but usually a leghold is best here. If there's an obvious haul-out, set the trap a couple feet from the edge of the water about eight to ten inches below the water's surface. That sounds like the trap would be too far out and too deep, but an otter's body is long, and it usually comes to the bank chest-first. If your trap is too shallow or too close, you'll get a few glistening guard hairs and the otter will get a sore chest. Old trapping books advised using large, tooth-jawed traps to catch the otter by the chest, but modern trappers can't—and shouldn't—use these tactics. Just back off and deepen your trap location, and you'll connect with a hind foot.

I also use a three-hole dry set with good results at these toilet and rolling locations. Simply bed the trap firmly in the toilet area, and use a small log, rock, or clump of grass as a backing, with the trap pan about eight inches from the backing. Stake the trap securely and sift dirt, sand, or whatever is natural at the set over the trap. Punch three holes in a semi-circle above the trap—one under the front edge of the backing, and

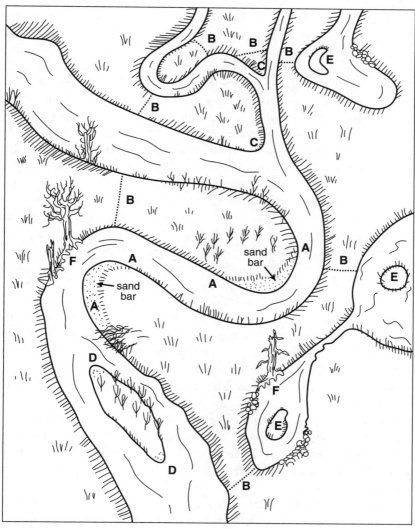

Likely otter set locations.

one to the left and right of the trap at a 45-degree angle. There are a few specific otter lures on the market, but otters are more indifferent to lure than other furbearers. I've had the most consistent results using Carman's Triple X predator lure in the center hole, with fish oil, chunks of fish, beaver castor lure, or mink gland lure in the side holes. Sometimes, if it's available at the set location, I'll place a fresh otter scat on the backing and give it a shot of red fox urine. If the toilet or rolling area is a large one, I'll usually make two of these sets six to eight feet apart, using different smells at each one.

Locations in the illustration marked "B" are overland crossings, where otters leave one waterway to travel to a different one, or short cuts across peninsulas from one section of stream to another. The main thing these crossovers have in common is that they are almost always at the narrowest stretch of land between the two water bodies. Remember that defining otter characteristic: he's a water animal that often comes to dry land. You can set these crossovers at either end with legholds or body-grippers, or anywhere along their length with legholds or (if legal) snares or body-grippers. For sets in the trail itself, pick natural pinch points where fallen trees, brush, or other obstructions narrow the travelway, as you would when trail-setting for other furbearers. You'll sometimes also find toilets and rolling areas at these locations.

If you're setting legholds in the water at either end of the trail, set the trap deep enough to miss the otter's chest. In many cases, the haul-outs are on relatively steep banks, so you don't have to set the trap back as far as when setting gently sloped sand bars. However, be sure the trap pan is at least eight inches deep to give the otter's chest plenty of clearance.

Those set locations marked "C" on the illustration are points of land where two streams come together. They're prime otter loafing and toilet areas, and can be set using the three-hole set described above. However, another hot location often overlooked by trappers is the very tip of the point. Otters will usually make landfall at the part that juts farthest into the water. Sometimes these points are rounded, and pinpointing the exact landing point is harder, but you can usually get away with a little fencing with brush or logs to narrow the possibilities. Just keep it looking natural, and don't be too heavy-handed. Depending on water depth at the point, the best trap location may be close to the bank (on a steep drop-off) or two to three feet out (on a shallow bar). Just be sure the pan is that minimum of eight inches deep.

Another excellent set for use at the junction of two streams sounds crude and amateurish, but it works. It requires clear water, a white or bright-colored bucket slotted to accept the springs of a body-gripper trap, the trap itself, a rock, and some tin foil. Wrap a fist-sized rock in aluminum foil and put it in the bottom of the bucket. Set the trap and fit the springs into the slots, and then run a wire or bungee cord from the back of one spring around the bottom of the trap to the back side of the other spring, to hold the trap firmly in the mouth of the bucket. Wire the chain to the bucket handle, add another longer length of wire to the handle, and then fill the bucket with water and lower it carefully to the bottom of the main waterway, close to the creek junction. Fasten the wire to a tree or bush so you can retrieve the bucket, trap and catch. This set works in practically any depth of water, but remember, the water must be clear so the otter can see it. It's a hard set to make, though, unless you're trapping from a boat.

"D" locations on the illustration are the upper and lower ends of islands in a stream with current. Sometimes the island's ends will be rounded, but in many cases they will come to a point, whittled sharp by passing current. Treat these set locations like the tributary points discussed in C.

Islands in still water ("E") usually don't have the sharp-nosed configuration of islands shaped by current. Even so, otters favor these small humps of terra firma surrounded by water. If an islet is being used, you'll find sign. You'll also probably find a favored landing area, which you can then set according to the depth and distance guidelines already mentioned. The bucket set described above is also good here.

"F" set locations are washed-out root systems of large trees (usually found along relatively steep banks on the outside bend of a stream) or large trees with hollow trunks and an opening at or near water level. Otters often use these places for temporary sleeping quarters or places to dine during their travels, and they make good set locations. Each of these places is different, so evaluate each and set it in the way you think best, with leg-holds, snares, or body-grippers.

The set location marked "G" is a logjam or large debris pile. You might find one almost anywhere, but usually they occur where floodwaters pile up against a shoreline. Otters use these piles the way they do the F locations, and they can be set in much the same way. Bucket sets are good choices at both F and G locations.

"H" is a small, sluggish waterway connecting two water bodies without any appreciable current. These are good for swim-through sets with snares or body-grippers, but they can be difficult to set because they're usually boggy and brush-choked.

However, when you find one of these connecting streams in good otter country, it pays to hitch up your waders, get out there and find some narrow spots to make swim-through sets. Since otters swim both above and below the surface, deciding how deep to place a snare or trap can be tough. One solution is to find a shallow place (no more than 12 to 18 inches) and lay a dive stick across the channel there. Then position the trap or snare on the bottom, directly beneath the dive stick.

GANG-SETTING

Whatever sets you use for otters, make several of them. Otters are very social animals, and they usually travel in pairs or small groups. Sometimes these are family groups, composed of a female and her pups from the previous breeding season. Sometimes the group is made of unrelated otters simply traveling together. Either way, if you only have one set at a particular location when the group passes through, you can only catch one of them. Make several sets and you'll collect some doubles and triples when they come through.

Don't let an absence of otter sign deter you from making sets in a good-looking area. Otters leave a lot of sign in some places, but sometimes they don't leave any more sign than an 18-wheeler does when it goes down the interstate.

Also, don't give up too quickly when your good-looking set locations don't pay off right away. Be patient, and leave your otter sets in place as long as possible. Remember that aggravating otter habit of taking a week or two to make a circuit of their route. The trapper's only defense against that is to wait 'em out, and if your sets are well maintained and in good locations, sooner or later they'll connect.

13

Beaver

Beavers aren't particularly wary or hard to trap, although some become trap-shy after escaping from poorly made sets. As with raccoons, the main problem most beginning trappers have with beavers isn't getting the animal into the trap, but keeping it there. Beavers are extremely strong, like fur-covered bulldozers, and they can make short work of getting out of an improperly staked, improperly set, or too-small trap.

Despite their strength, beavers have delicate front feet, and the "wrist" joints can dislocate very easily. Make your sets wrong, and a trapped beaver can simply power out of the trap, twist and roll until it wrings off the trapped toe (or even the entire front foot), pull the stake or break the wire and get away trap and all, or cut off a wooden trap stake and escape, again taking the trap with it.

TRAP SIZES AND STYLES

I've caught and held beavers by accident in number 1 and 1½ traps set for mink, muskrats, or raccoons, but use bigger stuff if you're targeting beavers. The 1.75 and 2 traps are barely adequate when set strictly for front-foot catches and surefire drowning sets, but beginners and veterans alike are better off using bigger traps.

My favorite beaver foothold traps are the number 5 Bridger longspring and the Montana Brand 750 coilspring. Both these traps have a 7½-inch jaw spread and get a high, firm grip on a beaver's front leg well above the fragile wrist joint. These big traps also easily accommodate the beaver's large, paddle-like hind foot.

Other suitable footholds for beavers include the Montana Brand 650 (6½ –inch jaw spread), number 3 and 4 longsprings, and number 3 and 4 coilsprings. Unless you're proficient at making consistent front-foot catches on beavers, don't use a trap with less than a 6-inch jaw spread.

Although the 220 body-gripper is strong enough to hold and kill the largest beaver, the 7-inch jaw spread is too small for most beaver trapping situations. They work well in tight passageways, but for most situations

Beaver trapping is fun and profitable, but when you start catching them in numbers, it can turn into hard work very fast.

you need more trap. The 330 body-gripper (10-inch jaw spread) is by far the most popular size with most beaver trappers, and the 280 (8-inch jaw spread) is a good compromise when otters are present and the trapper wishes to target them as well.

In recent years, a Canadian trap manufacturer came out with body-grippers with even larger jaw spreads, up to 12 inches. Also, some American entrepreneurs cut the jaws of their 330s and widen the jaw spread by welding extension rods to the jaws, creating traps with rectangular jaw spreads measuring 10 inches tall by 24 or more inches wide. All these large traps catch beavers, but personally, I've never seen a situation where I felt handicapped by having "only" a 330-size trap.

Snare cable used for beavers should be sturdy. Beaver snares can be made of cable as small as $5/64$ when rigged for drowning, but $3/32$ or even $1/8$ is a better choice in sets where drowning isn't an option.

Likewise, trappers using tie wire for fastening beaver traps and snares should be cautious when using smaller wire. Cable makes more dependable slide drowner material, but 9-, 11-, or 12-gauge wire can be used if it's replaced when it gets kinked after making a catch. When forced to use wire smaller than 12 gauge, double the wire and twist it tightly along the entire length of the drowner, forming a "rope" of wire that doesn't have any loops or gaps.

The number 5 longspring, with its 7½-inch jaw spread, is one of the best all-around foothold traps for beaver. But even with these big traps, surefire drowning sets are required.

A concrete building block makes a good weight for the bottom end of a beaver slide wire drowner. This photo shows three good ways to fasten the drowner to the cable, using an S-hook on the cable to attach it to the block. Top: doubled 12-gauge or 14-gauge wire; center: 2/0 trap chain; bottom: ³/₃₂ snare cable.

DROWNING METHODS

Strictly speaking, beavers don't drown. According to researchers, what they actually do is hold their breath until they suffocate. However, in these pages we'll call it drowning.

Every beaver trapper's goal with every foothold set should be to get the beaver into a surefire drowning situation as quickly as possible after the animal sticks its foot into the trap. Because of the beaver's strength and its ability to quickly chew through many obstacles, simple drowning methods like tangle stakes don't work well. The only reliable drowning method is with a one-way slider on a wire leading from the set location to water deep enough to drown a beaver. For a front-foot catch, this is about 2½ feet; for a hind-foot catch, double that depth. A weight of about 25 to 30 pounds is sufficient, but make sure the slide wire or cable is straight and tight between the shallow-water stake and the drowning weight or drowning stake.

FOOTHOLD SETS FOR BEAVERS

The number one foothold set for beavers is the scent mound set, also called the mud-pie set or the castor mound set. Beavers are both colonial and territorial animals, and they mark their territories by pushing up piles of bottom muck and debris onto the bank at the edge of the water and depositing scent from their anal glands on the pile. They do this at irregular intervals throughout their home ranges, and where the territories of two or more colonies come together, the amount of castor mound activity can be amazing.

The castor mound set can be made at existing mounds, or created from scratch by piling up a softball-size gob of bottom mud and muck at a suitable place and smearing a pea-size gob of castor-based beaver lure on the pile. Sometimes it's not necessary to use the lure when making a set at an existing mound, but it's still a good idea because it makes the beaver work the set more aggressively.

Bed the trap in the edge of the water in front of the castor mound, an inch or so beneath the surface, with the pan of the trap about two or three inches off center to allow for the beaver's wide body. Drive a stake completely into the mud beside the set and run the slide wire out to deep water. As an added touch, many trappers peel a couple of twigs and place the white sticks at the mound for added visual attraction.

If the water is shallow for a little way out from the bank, the set is complete at this point because the beaver will be wading and walking when it hits the trap. However, if the shoreline breaks off quickly to deep water, a beaver approaching the mound may hit the bank with its chest,

This beaver was taken at a simple castor mound set made on an open bank where a small stream entered a larger bayou. The castor mound is visible on the bank.

with its front legs still tucked under. This is undesirable, because the beaver will spring the trap and not be caught and may develop a wariness that makes it hard to catch in future castor mound sets.

In this case, cut two or three half-inch sticks a foot or so long, sharpen them on one end, and stick them in the bottom beside or in front of the trap, with the sharp points just under water and positioned so that the beaver will hit them with its chest before it reaches the trap. When the beaver's chest touches the sticks, the animal will puts its feet down and will hit the trap properly for a good catch.

Beaver runs (often called "beaver slides," although that's not what they are) that go from the water level up onto a stream or lake bank are also good locations for foothold sets, provided you use the poke-stick trick when the water is too deep at the base of the run. Likewise, beavers often develop heavily used crossovers between adjacent bodies of water, such as between a stream and a nearby lake, or across a levee separating two ponds or reservoirs. These crossovers are often good for two sets, one on each end.

On practically every beaver dam, there will be a crossover trail where beavers cross the dam going both ways, upstream and downstream. Usually, these are located near the center of the dam, or at the center of the stream if the dam lies more on one side of the stream than

Beavers are easily captured in snares set in slides and runways going up creek or lake banks. Be sure to stake the snare solidly.

the other. Effective foothold sets can be made at these crossovers, on both the upstream and downstream side. In many cases, though, the water on the downstream side will be too shallow for effective drowning, in which case a body-gripper or snare may be a better choice.

Float sets can sometimes be used to good advantage for beavers, particularly on streams or lakes where water levels fluctuate daily. The float is made similar to a muskrat float except that the scale is considerably larger. Two logs about 12 inches in diameter and 6 feet long, connected in a V shape by a couple pieces of scrap lumber, is about right. The float should be big enough to support the heavy beaver trap and an 8 x 8 x 16 concrete block, which will serve as the drowning weight. Place the block at the rear of the V, and pile a handful of bottom muck on the block and lure it as when making a castor mound set. Fasten the trap to the block, the block to the float and the float to a secure object that won't float away when the water rises.

One other foothold set some trappers use with success is tearing out a small section of a beaver dam and setting the trap in the break. The idea is that the beaver will get caught when it comes to repair the damage, and this sometimes works. But all too often, what happens is that the trapper comes back the next day and finds the dam freshly repaired, with his trap incorporated into the repair. The advice from this corner is to use your foothold traps at castor mounds and the other sets described above, and leave the dams intact.

SNARES AND BODY-GRIPPER SETS

When using body-grippers for beavers, the trap may be completely submerged, partially submerged, or all the way out of the water on dry land. However, many states restrict the use of large body-grippers to water sets, and the definition of what constitutes a water set varies from state to state. In some states, the trap must be completely submerged, and in others part of the trap may be above water. Regardless of the trapping regulations, though, any trapper who uses beaver-size body-grippers should use them carefully, because these traps are perfectly capable of killing pets and livestock.

Beavers often dig travelway channels in streambeds, in beaver ponds, and extending from beaver ponds for some distance into flat farmland or woodlands. Many of these swim channels are perfect places for body-gripper traps. Simply position the trap in the swim channel, brace it securely, and you're finished. If the water is more than a few inches over the trap, you may want to position a dive stick directly over the trap, crossways to the channel, to make a surface-swimming beaver dive under it and hit the trap.

Underwater den entrances make good body-gripper locations, whether they're at bank dens or on beaver lodges, but unless the water is clear these are hard to find. Even in clear water, they can be so far beneath the surface they're almost impossible to set. Some trapping supply manufacturers make long-handled body-gripper trap stabilizers that can be used to position traps over deep dens, and sometimes it's possible to use two long poles through the springs or spring eyes to lower the trap and position it properly. Usually, though, the best option when you're faced with a deep-water den entrance is to forget about it and catch the beavers elsewhere.

If you have a choice in the matter, body-grippers are almost always a better choice than snares because the trap kills the animal quickly. Beavers fight snares hard, and the cable usually causes pelt damage. However, snares are effective beaver-catching tools, and they definitely have a place on most beaver lines. If you are walking a considerable distance to reach the set location, snares are advantageous because they're light and you can carry many of them without trouble. And in many states, snares are legal for use out of water, while large body-grippers are not. Snares are also safer for pets and can often be used in places where body-grippers would cause too much danger for dogs and cats.

There are many types of locking devices used on snares today, but the most common is the bent washer lock. This lock is effective, easy to make, and inexpensive. You can use more expensive and more complicated snare locks, but you won't find one that's any better.

Snares can be used in practically any situation where body-grippers are used, but where they really shine is on beaver runs and slides on open banks where there's little brush or vegetation in which to camouflage a body-gripper. Snares are very inconspicuous, and if beavers notice them at all, they probably think the snare cable is a vine or stick.

The two most important things about setting snares, other than the obvious one of setting them in the right place, are using the proper loop diameter and stabilizing the snare so it will close on the beaver as the animal tries to pass through.

For most beavers, a loop size of about eight to nine inches is appropriate. Some jumbo individuals may require a larger loop size, but not many. The eight- to nine-inch loop will allow most beavers to get their head and one or both front legs through the loop and will catch them around the rib cage. If you're catching beavers by the hips or even by the tail, your loops are probably too big.

There are many ways of stabilizing beaver snares. One of the simplest and most effective is sticking a piece of cane or a sturdy, straight twig into

The five locks at the top of this photo are all effective when used on slide-wire drowning rigs. The four assorted washers at the bottom of the photo are snare locks, and they can also serve double duty as slide-wire drowner locks.

the ground beside the trail, angling the stick over the trail, then wiring the snare to the stick using a 6-inch length of 16-gauge wire. The support stick does double duty, also serving as an obstacle to make the beaver lower its head and pass through the loop. Snares can also be stabilized with stiff wire bent into a series of tight loops. Weave the cable through the loops and stick the wire into the ground or twist it around a nearby bush. These two methods will work at almost all snare set locations.

DON'T OVERSET

One mistake of many inexperienced beaver trappers is making too many sets in one area. Because of their lifestyles and size, beavers leave a lot of sign, and it's easy to overestimate the number of animals present in an area. In most cases, a beaver colony consists of no more than six or seven animals, and unless you're doing nuisance control work, you don't want to catch them all and wipe out the breeding stock.

In most instances, making two or three good sets at a colony will allow you to take all the animals you need to take from that spot in two or three days, at which time it's wise to pull the traps and move on to another area.

14

Coyote, Gray Fox, Bobcat, and Red Fox

As the previous chapters illustrate, there are considerable differences in effective techniques for the water-associated furbearers. There are some differences in effective techniques for the four upland predators we're going to discuss in this chapter, too, but there are more similarities than differences.

The red fox is more a creature of open land than the coyote, bobcat, and gray fox. Bobcats are more sight-oriented and curious than the three canines, and are "dumber" when it comes to traps. Gray foxes are more single-minded when they're traveling, and are harder to lure to a slightly off-location set than are coyotes, cats, and reds. Coyotes are stronger by far than grays, reds, or bobcats. Warier, too.

That paragraph just about sums up the differences in these four upland furbearers.

The similarities, though, go on and on. All four species feed on much the same things, although coyotes and grays eat far more vegetable matter than do reds and cats. All four travel basically the same trails when they occupy the same habitat. All four are basically nocturnal, all four frequently travel in pairs or larger groups, all four work sets in more or less the same manner, and all four are susceptible to the same basic trapping techniques. Therefore, to avoid the repetition that would be inevitable if each of these four species of upland predator had its own chapter, we're going to cover them all here, discussing differences in technique for each species when necessary.

First, remember the clean trapping issue. The three wild canines have noses that are literally thousands of times more sensitive than yours, and while the bobcat doesn't have olfactory abilities of that caliber, its nose is still many times better than a human's. It's impossible to keep from leaving some human odor at your sets for these animals, so there's no sense in being too paranoid about it. But don't get careless, either. The best

Red fox

Bobcat

Gray fox

Coyote

course of action is to use clean equipment and clean traps, minimize contamination when you can, and then don't worry about it.

Second, don't go overboard on traps at a set location, but don't short yourself either. Remember that pairing or group tendency exhibited so often by cats, coons, and canines. If a location is worth one predator set, it's usually worth two. Maybe three.

TRAP SIZES AND STYLES

Obviously, coyotes are larger and stronger than foxes. Bobcats, though not much stronger than foxes, have larger feet. Therefore, if you're trapping exclusively for coyotes or bobcats, number 3 longspring or coilspring traps would be a good choice. But there are also grays, reds, and raccoons on most upland traplines, and big traps are unfriendly to the delicate feet and leg bones of these smaller animals.

On my upland predator trapline, I'm targeting all five species, and whichever one gets to the set first is the one I want to catch. That's why I use one trap and one trap only when I'm setting for upland predators, and that trap is a 1¾ coilspring, with the factory springs removed and replaced with number 3 coilsprings. This trap has a 5⅜-inch jaw spread, which makes it an acceptable compromise for those big-footed bobcats,

If coyotes or bobcats are the only likely catch, the number 3 longspring and number 3 coilspring traps (at top) are good choices. However, if gray foxes, red foxes, or raccoons are present, a better choice is the 1¾ coilspring, beefed up with number 3 coilsprings. The versatile snare, where legal, is good for all upland predators.

Snares for upland predators are most effective when set in travelway bottle- necks, such as this gap in a cedar tree that had fallen across a woods road.

and with the larger springs it's plenty of trap for the strongest coyote. I shorten the chain to three double links, with an extra box swivel in the chain.

Snares are excellent upland predator catchers, too, although of course loop size and height of the snare loop must be adjusted depending on which of the upland furbearers you're after. I sometimes use $^3/_{32}$ snare cable for coyotes, but $^5/_{64}$ is also a good choice. I prefer $^5/_{64}$ cable for reds, grays, cats, and coons.

For coyotes, the best loop size is about 10 inches, with the bottom of the loop 8 to 10 inches off the ground. For bobcats, an 8- or 9-inch loop is usually best, with the bottom of the loop about 6 to 8 inches off the ground. For both reds and grays, the loop should be no bigger than 7 inches (6 inches is probably better), with the bottom of the loop about 6 inches above the ground. For raccoons, as mentioned previously, the proper loop size is 6 to 7 inches, with the bottom of the loop about 4 inches above the ground.

These dimensions and distances are, of course, approximate. On steep slopes, loop distances above ground should be a third lower than on level ground, and heavy brush or overhanging obstacles can affect the proper height for all the above species. For snare sets made for a variety of species, splitting the difference is usually in order.

No matter what furbearer you're after and no matter what cable size you use, set your snares in narrowed-down places in the trail or in grassy or brushy areas for best results. A snare looks like a vine to a furbearer, but if it's mixed in with other vines and bushes they'll be less likely to avoid it.

LOCATION IS EVERYTHING

As with sets for any other furbearer, sets for upland predators must be right on target to be effective. Fortunately, it's not difficult to learn to read the landscape and pick out the high-percentage set locations. Here are some examples:

1. Any small clearing in a wooded area is a magnet for foxes, bobcats, and coyotes, as well as raccoons and other terrestrial furbearers. The clearing may be a food plot, a log landing from a previous timber-harvesting operation, a natural opening, or even the yard of a seldom-used hunting cabin. In most cases, the best set location for this particular opening is where the woods road enters the opening, although a close examination might reveal other natural travelways entering or leaving the opening that would also make good set locations.

2. If there's a tree or small cluster of trees or saplings in a field, pasture, or food plot, by all means make a set or two near it. For whatever reason, predators (especially canines and raccoons) seem almost compelled to check out these trees.

3. The junctures of woods roads and game trails are also hot set locations for an obvious reason: your target animals will probably be traveling both trails, and sets made here will be in the travelway of animals using either one.

4. Sharp bends in woods roads or trails often make good set locations, because the animals traveling them usually crowd the inside of the bend to save themselves a few steps. Furbearers are like people; they take shortcuts when they can. Sets made near the inside track of a two-track woods road as it goes around a curve are almost sure to be right in the animal's path.

Eye appeal is just as important for upland predators as it is for water-associated furbearers. A lone tree in a pasture, a single hay bale left in a field, a large rock, a tree stump, an old abandoned piece of farm machinery—all of these things and more can serve as the basis for sets with good eye appeal.

5. Gaps in fences where field roads or trails pass through are usually hot locations, whether they're in the open or in the woods. These are similar in principle to setting the entranceway to food plots and forest openings as discussed in 1 above, but here there's an added advantage—the gap in the fence tends to funnel the target animals even tighter. Never pass up a location like this without examining it closely for sign.

6. Field and pasture corners act as furbearer funnels for animals skirting the edge of the openings. More often than not, you'll find one or more trails leading under the fence and into a field at its corners. These make excellent locations for snares as well as footholds.

7. Likewise, you'll often find a trail leading through the narrowest part of the woods or brush where two openings or fields are fairly close together. Even if there's not a visible trail at such locations, sets made in either or both openings right where the cover is narrowest will probably produce.

8. Weedy or brushy fencerows between fields are good travelways for predators, and anywhere along such a field border might make a good set. The highest-percentage locations, however, are at the ends,

where the fencerow meets another fence, a ditch or stream, or other field border.

9. High banks along streams make excellent predator set locations, especially for bobcats. Whether it's a mud bank rising six feet above the water level or a rocky bluff towering several hundred feet, these high places are among the best cat locations you'll ever find—and they're not too shabby for canines and coons, either.

10. After you've set up the high bluff, don't neglect to take a look at the low bank beneath the bluff, as well as the sand bar or mud bar that can usually be found straight across the stream from the high bank. These make better coon set locations than anything else, but you'll also pick up a few canines and cats here as well—particularly on the bluff bank side of the stream.

11. Almost every trapper knows a beaver dam or log spanning a stream is a good place to catch a mink or coon, but these are predator highways as well. A dam is a great place to hang a snare or two, and

Set the edge for predators of all types. The border between two types of habitat (brush and open field, row crop and woods, rocky bluff and smooth, flat creek bottom) will almost always be a well-used travelway for a variety of upland predators.

    the landings at either end of the dam make excellent dirt hole set locations.

12. The manmade dams of stock ponds are good predator locations, although livestock can sometimes be a problem here. Predators not only water at these places, but they also seem to favor the top of an earthen dam for a toilet location.

13. The intermittent or seasonally dry streambed below a stock pond is often a highway for predators as well, since there's more cover here and predators use these dry streambeds for travelways.

14. Hay bales, haystacks, old stumps, abandoned vehicles or farm implements, or other solitary objects surrounded by open fields have the same drawing power for predators as the solitary trees discussed in point 2 above. You won't find sign at every one, but you'll find it at many of them.

15. Rocky ledges, cliffs, and broken areas of rock, especially if they're in or near thick brush, are magnets for bobcats, and provide likely set locations for the other upland furbearers as well, except for red fox.

    As you can see, it doesn't require a lot of deep thinking to look at a chunk of countryside and pick out the best places to set for predators. Just examine the landscape, use your head, think like a predator, make efficient, mechanically sound sets . . . and start raking in the fur.

THE GENERIC PREDATOR SET
The number of possible sets that will work for upland predators is staggering. If a trapper made just one of each type of predator set that's been described in trapping books like this one, he'd need a thousand traps to get the job done. That's fine if you want to do things that way, but there's no need. Remember the K.I.S.S. philosophy. All you need to catch any of the upland predators is one type of set, made the same way every time.

    The generic predator set is simple, versatile and inconspicuous. Basically, it's a blended-in flat set, with no dirt pattern to attract unwanted human attention. Keep the prevailing wind direction in mind, and make the set very close to, but on the upwind side of, the track you think your target animals will be walking. In most parts of the country, the prevailing wind is west, southwest, or northwest, but hills, tree lines, stream courses, valleys, and other natural landscape features can alter the prevailing wind direction at individual locations. Alter your trap placement accordingly. If you're not sure, or if unsettled weather means shifting winds, make one set on each side of the anticipated travelway.

    Choose a low backing such as a clump of grass, a fist-size rock or a small log, on a level spot or on a slight incline, no more than 5 to 10

Not much backing is required—or desirable—at a generic predator set. The important things are keeping the angle of the hole fairly steep, setting on a slight incline, bedding the trap firmly, and, of course, setting on precisely the right location.

degrees. Move a backing into position if necessary. Using a rebar stake, punch a hole four to six inches deep under the edge of your backing, on the downhill side or on the side from which you think the animal will approach. Make the hole at a fairly steep angle, but not vertical—20 degrees is about right. Dig a trap bed in front of the hole just big enough and deep enough to accommodate your trap. Stake the trap with a rebar or disposable stake driven into the trap bed. Next, bed the trap firmly, placing the pan about six inches out from the hole and offset an inch or two to one side. Sift dirt over the trap to cover it, and then run a little surface duff through the sifter to blend in the trap bed. Use whatever is natural at the set location—grass, cedar needles, or dead leaves.

Make the trap bed as small as possible. Digging larger holes is more time-consuming, and a larger, deeper trap bed makes for softer dirt around the trap, which can lead to digging if the animal misses the pan and steps onto the softer dirt first.

Lure choice is a matter of personal preference. However, in keeping with the K.I.S.S. philosophy, keep your lure selection to a minimum. Experimentation is fine, and no trapper should ever hesitate to try a new lure, but using a different smell at each set just to change things up is overkill. I use two primary lures at generic predator sets, because as mentioned, I usually make two sets at each location. I think the different smells are an advantage when sets are close. On the infrequent occasions when I make three sets at one location, I use a third lure (or just urine alone) for the third set.

Don't use too much lure, especially if it's a loud, call-type lure with a skunk component. Using too much loud lure often causes canines to roll on the set, and you won't catch many by the scruff of the neck. A couple drops on a dry stick is plenty, and be sure to poke it well down in the hole to make it hard for the animal to reach.

As with lures, simplicity is the ticket when adding urine to sets. Many trappers don't bother with urine at all, but I feel it helps as a suspicion remover and gives the animal something else to think about when approaching the set. The best choice of urine, in most instances, is red fox.

This is because there's a pecking order in the blood-and-guts real world of predators and prey. Wolves and cougars are on top, of course, but in most areas the top-end predator is the coyote. Then comes bobcat, then gray fox, then red fox. Since red fox urine is the least threatening to the members of this descending pecking order, it's the logical choice.

Some trappers spray a mist of urine over the entire set, but this is a mistake because it calls the animal's attention to the area where the trap is located. You want his attention focused beyond the trap, not on it. Therefore, squirt a light stream (not a mist) of urine directly onto the backing, above the lure and beyond the trap.

Many trappers use both bait and lure at sets like this, but this is unnecessary and can lead to problems with rodents, birds, and other unwanted critters. It also makes the set much more attractive to possums and skunks, and this you do not need. The lure and the urine are attractant enough. Leave it at that, and K.I.S.S.

OTHER TYPES OF DIRT HOLE SETS

The generic predator set described above is a low-profile version of the extremely popular dirt hole set. Sometimes, though, it's an advantage to make a set that has more visual appeal. That's where the standard dirt hole set comes in.

This set is made in the same locations described above for the generic predator set, and the set construction itself is pretty much the same except for the hole and for the blended-in trap bed. In the standard dirt hole set, the hole is two to four inches across and eight inches to a foot deep, and the dirt from the hole is spread in a highly visible, fan-shaped

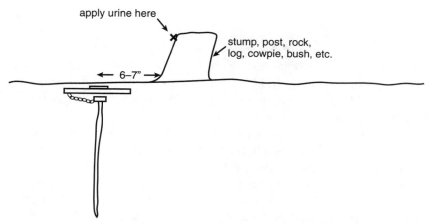

The urine post set is a good variation to use when making a third set at high-use predator locations.

pattern over the concealed and carefully bedded trap. Lure and urine application are the same. This set is a good choice where furbearer populations haven't been subjected to much trapping pressure and where theft is unlikely.

URINE POST SETS

Canines especially, but also bobcats, leave calling cards along their route in the form of little squirts of pee on convenient objects—rocks, the end of a log, isolated clumps of grass, bushes. Sometimes a canine will scratch the dirt with its hind feet after using the urine post, and the trapper can find the location that way. However, it's not really necessary to find an existing urine post, because you can create one almost anywhere canines are traveling.

Simply choose a likely looking object (or put one in place where you want it) and bed a trap in front, blending it carefully with material natural to the immediate area. If you're importing an object to serve as a scent station, a dried cow patty is a good choice in cattle country. Also, a charred, blackened piece of wood about eight to ten inches long, driven into the ground a third of the way, is for some reason very hard to beat. Whatever you use, the pan of your trap should be seven to eight inches from the urine post, directly in front. This will take all three canines most of the time. No other lure or bait is necessary.

Urine post sets are useful as the third set in high-traffic locations, and they also shine when used near a bucket set to take those curious canines that fidget and fiddle around a bucket but won't enter it.

REMAKES

One of the advantages of using the generic predator set, in addition to its effectiveness on all upland furbearers, is that it's an inconspicuous set. In high-theft areas, this is important. However, once you've made a catch, there'll be a catch circle, and the inconspicuous nature of the set is gone. If theft likelihood is high, you may not want to reset at that location. If you do, though, here are a few guidelines.

Replace all the hardware, including the stake. Everything is going to be contaminated with the odor of the trapped animal, and this destroys the advantage of the blended-in trap bed. Next, don't reset inside the catch circle. Move at least a few inches outside the circle for the remake. The circle is going to be attractive to other furbearers, and you want to take advantage of that. But the smell of the previous catch is going to permeate the entire circle, and there's no surefire way to effectively focus the next animal's attention on a specific few square inches of that circle, which is what you have to do to catch the animal.

By moving barely outside the circle, you'll solve the focusing problem and still be able to use the catch circle for an attractor. I prefer to use a different lure at this remake, not because I think the original lure wouldn't be effective, but because the old lure odor is also permeating the catch circle. The new lure provides something different for the next furbearer to check out. I also sometimes go ahead and make a standard dirt hole set for the remake, since my cover is blown at that location anyway.

BLIND SETS

Many good predator trappers use a lot of blind sets, setting footholds in trails and runs being used by furbearers. Trail sets like this will take a lot of fur, but they have a couple of built-in disadvantages—the trapper has only one shot at catching the target animal when it comes through, and many other animals besides furbearers also use these trails.

To make an effective trail set, the trapper must know with some degree of certainty exactly where the target animal will step, and position the pan of a well-concealed trap under that precise spot. Sometimes there are natural obstacles in a trail or run that will make a furbearer step in a precise spot, and other times the trapper can add a guide stick or two, or a few well-placed pebbles or small rocks, to encourage the animal to step on the trap pan. Don't get too heavy-handed, though, or the animal will usually go around.

I do use a few blind sets every year on my upland predator line, but in a vast majority of cases, I find that a generic predator set close beside the trail is a better choice.

FREEZE-PROOFING DIRT SETS

Dirt sets, under most conditions, won't freeze unless the temperature drops to 25 degrees or below and stays there for the entire night. In most cases, weather that consists of daily highs in the 40s and 50s and nightly lows in the 20s doesn't present any freeze-up problem for the dirt trapper. The soil retains enough warmth under these conditions to keep from freezing, especially in the first half of the night when most furbearer movement takes place.

But when things get colder, dirt sets can be effectively freeze-proofed by sprinkling the bottom of the trap bed lightly with flaked calcium chloride or plain table salt, then adding more chloride or salt to your sifter and mixing that with the dirt as you cover and bed your trap. Calcium chloride is available at home supply warehouse stores and concrete companies. If you have dirt sets already made when cold weather moves in, sprinkling chloride or salt on top of the dirt pattern will also work, but is not quite as effective because it doesn't penetrate as well to the dirt beneath the trap.

Flaked calcium chloride or plain table salt are both good anti-freeze materials, but don't use them unless you're sure you're going to need them.

Although both salt and calcium chloride are odorless, they both also attract and absorb moisture out of the soil and air, and the trap set will take on a wet-looking appearance considerably different from its surroundings. This wet spot doesn't seem to bother most furbearers, although undoubtedly some animals do refuse the set. For this reason, and because both salt and especially calcium chloride are very corrosive, don't use this freeze-proofing method unless you must, and make sure you only use traps that have been well waxed. After making a catch, take the trap home and wash it thoroughly, or you'll wind up with a rust ball.

BUCKETS FOR BOBCATS

The baited bucket guarded with a 160 or 220 body-gripper is also effective on bobcats if the bucket is set in the right location. You may also catch an occasional gray or red fox in buckets, but don't depend on a bucket line to keep your fox stretchers full.

Stay close to rocky ledges and brushy thickets when you target bobcats with buckets. Any overhanging ledge is worth a close look. ATV or Jeep roads through grassy or brushy clear cuts or pine plantations are also excellent bobcat bucket locations. Throwing an armload of twigs, leaves, or grass over the bucket to form a sort of cubby isn't a bad idea. You can accomplish the same cubby effect by snugging the bucket among the low-hanging limbs of a cedar or other small conifer.

When targeting bobcats with buckets, stay close to the thickets and rocky areas bobcats prefer. Use bait with fur or feathers attached, and brush in your buckets for best results.

Using fish for bait is acceptable, but I've found that bait with feathers or fur on it is better for cats, probably because of the added sight attraction. Roadkill is fine; the bobcat won't care as long as it's fresh. A piece of surveyor's flagging hung above the bucket can help pull in bobcats to your sets, and so can a skunky, long-distance call lure on a bush or tree trunk above your set. However, if you're on location with your sets, the flagging and call lure are probably unnecessary.

Although it's rarely necessary for coons, fastening the bait in the back of your buckets is important for trapping the much longer-legged bobcat. This can be easily accomplished by drilling two ⅛-inch holes in the back of the bucket and running a 18-inch piece of wire through the holes into the interior of the bucket. Wrap a turn or two of wire around your bait, or poke the wire through the bait. This accomplishes three things: it makes it impossible for a furbearer to rake the bait out without getting caught, raises the bait and makes it more visible, and makes the bait harder to reach for the rodents that are also inevitably attracted to it.

Another way to set buckets for bobcats (coons, too) is by using two buckets instead of one, with the bottoms removed from both buckets. Cut one bucket an inch or two up from the bottom, so the opening will be slightly larger. Notch the tops of the buckets to accommodate the springs of your body-grippers, and slide the buckets together bottom-to-bottom, telescope fashion. Put bait in the middle of the bucket tunnel you've just created, set a trap in each end, and you've not only created a good bobcat set, but given yourself a chance for a double, if not on bobcats then perhaps on coons.

Never rely solely on a bucket to cover a set location. Although coyotes will almost never stick their heads in a bucket, and gray and red fox will do so only occasionally, canines are still attracted to buckets and will prowl around close by while they investigate this strange, good-smelling thing. A big-pattern dirt-hole set or a urine post set close by will take a lot of these canines—and sometimes a bucket-refusing bobcat as well. Gang setting is an important part of high-efficiency trapping, no matter what type of sets you use.

DON'T GET TOO FANCY

The whole key to efficient dry-land trapping is to not get too elaborate with your set making. Simple sets work just as well as and usually better than complicated ones, and they take much less time to make and tend.

Less bother means less time spent at each set, which means more time available, which equals more sets in the ground, larger catches, and more money for your efforts at season's end. That's an equation every trapper can live with.

15

The Lowly Ones: Skunk and Opossum

In most cases, the problem trappers have with skunks and opossums isn't catching them, it's avoiding them. These two furbearers are very common in most parts of the country, and both are strongly attracted to bait of almost any sort. They live in the same habitats and travel the same trails used by the more desirable furbearers, both in the dry uplands and along watercourses. What trapper hasn't had the experience of approaching a prime bobcat, fox, coyote, or mink set with high hopes, only to find a grinning possum or woods kitty in the trap?

It wouldn't be so bad if possum and skunk pelts were valuable, but both animals are usually on the low end of the commercial scale. In recent years, it's taken a very big, very pale, very prime possum pelt to bring three dollars, and smaller, darker, less prime specimens are virtually worthless. Many trappers feel it's more trouble to handle skunks and possums than they're worth. Skunks are usually a little more valuable than possums in the specialty market, and skunk musk is in demand in the lure-making industry, but the slightly higher price doesn't compensate for the obvious problems inherent in dealing with trapped skunks.

Even so, it's still sometimes advantageous to set traps specifically for possums and skunks, if for no other reason than to catch them before they can find and blunder into sets made for higher-priced animals.

TRAP SIZES AND STYLES
Neither possums nor skunks are strong or fast, and the number 0 or 1 single longsprings are both adequate. But since any foothold trap set for possum or skunk could also connect with a larger, stronger, more desirable furbearer, it's usually a good idea to use larger traps. The 1½ and 1¾ coilsprings are both good, as are number 2 longsprings. These traps will also hold most of the larger furbearers as well.

Body-grippers in sizes 110, 120, 160, and 220 are all suitable for possum and skunk trapping, but both animals are frequently found alive

The bane of the upland predator trapper. While large possums like this one may bring two or three dollars, smaller specimens are virtually worthless.

The other bane of the upland trapper. Skunks have a decent value in the specialty market, but most trappers feel the money isn't worth the smell.

when caught in 110s. This isn't much of a problem if the catch is a possum; it can get a little hairy if you're dealing with a live, angry skunk.

EFFECTIVE SETS

As already mentioned, possums and skunks are suckers for bait sets. This is one of the biggest reasons I almost never use bait when I'm trapping for other furbearers. But if I'm setting for other critters in a high-traffic area for skunks and possums, I often make two or three additional sets in the vicinity (usually 50 to 100 feet away from the main set) in an attempt to shortstop these undesirables before they can get to my better sets. For bait, I use fish, spoiled flesh, or other loud-smelling items such as canned sardines, jack salmon, or canned cat food.

I use two basic foothold sets for possums and skunks. One is the standard dirt hole, made as described in the previous chapter. The other is a cubby-type set made by constructing a small enclosure of brush, rocks, logs, or other natural material, putting bait at the back of the enclosure, and concealing the trap in front. Sometimes I'll use a discarded coffee can or shortening can as the cubby, putting a few rocks or small logs around it to hold it in place.

Don't get sloppy with your set construction. Possums and skunks will often step in an uncovered trap, and I doubt there's any way you could leave enough foreign odor around a set to deter these animals, but these secondary sets sometimes attract bobcats and canines. Therefore,

Good traps for possums and skunks. If this photo looks familiar, it should: the same traps that are effective for muskrats are also good possum and skunk catchers.

*Baited box cubbies made of scrap 1x6 lumber and guarded with 110
body-grippers will short-stop a lot of possums and skunks, but these
are bulky and can call unwanted attention to your trapline activities.
For bait, cheap canned cat food is hard to beat.*

proper trap bedding and all the other things discussed in previous chapters is just as important at possum and skunk sets as it is at sets made
for more wary furbearers. If you start taking shortcuts with your possum
and skunk sets, you'll be running the very real risk of educating the animals you really want to catch.

Bucket sets are good possum and skunk takers, too, using the same
techniques used for bucketing coons. Body-grippers set in trails and dens
will account for a lot of possums and skunks as well. If there are abandoned farm buildings or houses near your other sets, or hay barns and
other similar farm buildings, clustering a few bait sets and bucket sets
around them can go a long way toward reducing your skunk and possum problem in the area. Old buildings are very attractive den sites for
possums and especially skunks.

Cage traps are also effective for possums and skunks, and catching them in cages usually eliminates the odor problem when trapping
skunks. When setting cage traps for these animals, it's wise to drape an
old blanket or piece of tarp or cloth over the trap, with a slit cut in the
cloth for the carrying handle to stick through. Not only does this create a
tunnel effect and make the trap more inviting, but it also allows the trapper to approach the trap from the side and remain out of sight of a
trapped skunk. You can then carefully lift the trap and carry it to your
truck or to a nearby body of water.

16

Dealing with Live Catches

One of the least enjoyable parts of trapping is the necessity of killing live animals in traps. Most trappers take every opportunity to make drowning-type sets or other lethal sets so the trapped animal will die quickly after becoming caught. A quick death for the animal is more humane, and it also reduces the risk of theft, wring-outs, pelt damage, and depredation by other furbearers or raptors. It's just better all around.

But not all of them are dead when we arrive. Sometimes a trapped animal refuses to go down a slide wire, or it hangs up and can't go down the wire, or a body-gripper gets a bad strike and the animal is still alive in the trap. And, of course, when making dry sets for coons and upland predators, the animal is almost always still alive in the trap. Therefore, the trapper must be prepared to kill these animals in a humane and efficient manner.

Shooting furbearers in the head with a .22 rifle or pistol, using shorts or CB caps, is the most common dispatching method for most trappers. The best place to put the bullet is high between the eyes and at a fairly steep downward angle, into the main part of the brain. For side shots, right into the ear canal is good.

Shooting works well, and it is the only safe and humane method I've found for killing trapped beavers, otters, raccoons, and coyotes. Still, there are problems associated with it. For one obvious thing, the gunfire can attract unwanted attention to the trapper's activities, and this can lead to problems down the road. Another problem with shooting trapped furbearers is that head wounds bleed profusely, even when the animal dies instantly, and often the result is a lot of blood on the fur. This must be removed or it will devalue the pelt. To minimize blood on the pelt, pick the animal up by a hind foot as soon as you're sure it is dead and hold it off the ground, so the blood won't get on the pelt as badly.

Both red and gray foxes can be easily, humanely, and bloodlessly killed by first tapping them between the eyes with a stout stick or long-handled trowel. While the animal is stunned, lay it on its side on firm

Despite our best efforts, sometimes drowning sets don't drown the animal. The trapper must always be equipped to either dispatch a target animal or release a nontarget one.

Gray and red foxes are easily and humanely killed by tapping them on the snout and then compressing the rib cage to stop the heart.

ground and step firmly on its rib cage, right behind the front leg. Put almost all your weight on that foot, and put your other foot on the animal's neck to keep it from biting you if it regains consciousness. In most cases, 30 seconds of foot pressure on the rib cage will stop the animal's heart and kill it very humanely.

Bobcats can be easily, humanely, and bloodlessly killed with a catchpole, a tool every trapper needs for releasing unwanted catches. A catchpole is a length of cable or stout rope fastened securely to one end of a four-foot length of metal or sturdy PVC pipe and threaded back through the pipe to form a noose on one end, with a locking device on the other end to prevent the loop from loosening. The trapper loops the noose over the trapped animal's head and pulls it firmly closed to restrain and control the animal while it is removed from the trap.

Bobcats can be easily and bloodlessly killed by using a catch pole to cut off their air supply. Unconsciousness comes in mere seconds, and death follows very shortly.

To use the catchpole to kill a bobcat, slip the noose over the cat's head and pull it down tightly. This will cut off the animal's air supply and render it unconscious in 10 to 15 seconds. Death usually comes in less than two minutes.

Muskrats and mink that are still alive in the trap can either be killed with a sharp rap on the head with a stick or trapper's trowel or by holding them under water with a stick until they drown. Drowning takes much longer for muskrats than for mink.

To kill a possum, carefully step on the trapped animal's head, grasp its tail, and remove it from the trap. Then, still holding the animal by its tail, lay it on the ground, chin and chest down, and step firmly on the head just behind the ears. Pull firmly upwards on the tail while exerting hard pressure with your foot, and you'll feel the neck vertebrae separate. This kills the possum instantly and painlessly.

Skunks are a problem. They almost always spray when they're shot in the head, and shooting them in the rib cage doesn't bring a quick kill and they sometimes spray anyway. Some trappers and trapping supply dealers sell skunk euthanasia kits consisting of two 5-foot lengths of pipe that fit together, with a bracket on one end to hold a hypodermic needle. The cylinder of the needle is filled with acetone, formalin, or some similar substance, and the trapper carefully and slowly approaches the trapped skunk, eases the needle into position, and slowly injects the liquid into the skunk's chest cavity. Reportedly, death is almost instantaneous, and the skunk does not spray.

Notice that I said reportedly in that last sentence. I have never tried this method, and I doubt I ever will. I have been sprayed by far too many skunks already, without giving any of them a shot at me on purpose. Although I have good friends in the trapping industry who swear it works, I'll leave this method to the more adventurous. I just shoot them in the head and then deal with the stink as best I can.

LIVE ANIMALS IN CAGE TRAPS

Cage-trapped animals can be shot, of course, but then you run the risk of damaging your trap. There are better ways. One is by asphyxiation or carbon monoxide poisoning. Carry the trap to the rear of a vehicle and cover it with a plastic tarp or heavy blanket. Run a short section of old garden hose into the exhaust pipe and stuff a piece of wet cloth around the hose to seal it off. Put the other end of the hose underneath the tarp, start the engine, and let it idle. Five minutes of this is usually enough to kill the animal.

Use the exhaust from your vehicle to quickly and humanely asphyxiate animals caught in cage traps. Submerging the entire trap in water is another quick and humane way to euthanize animals.

The other method is drowning. Simply carry the cage and the animal to a pond or stream and submerge it completely. Both of these are excellent methods for dealing with cage-trapped skunks. I've never had one spray yet when handled in this manner.

RELEASING UNWANTED CATCHES

Dogs, cats, out-of-season furbearers, unprime furbearers, and too-small furbearers sometimes get caught in traps set for other animals. Releasing them is fairly easy with a catchpole, as long as you're careful. Simply loop the noose of the pole around the animal's neck, pull it snug, push the animal back the length of the trap chain, and use your feet to depress the trap springs. Then loosen the noose and the animal will run away.

Occasionally, a dog will take exception to being caught and treated so shabbily and will want to press the issue. If a dog appears unusually aggressive when I approach to turn him loose, here's how I handle it: First, I drive my trapping vehicle as close as I can to the set location, and leave the driver's side door open. Then I remove the animal from the trap as described above, but keep the catch pole firmly on the animal while I walk backwards to my vehicle. I get in, close the door to a crack, and loosen the noose to release the dog. Usually even the most vicious dog will leave when it sees it can't get at you, but I had one dog that attacked my truck tires and followed me a half-mile down the road.

In the event I'm too far from my vehicle to use it as a safe haven, I'll apply a little extra pressure to the noose and cut off the dog's airway. I'm not trying to kill it; I just want to take the fight out of it. When it gets wobble-legged and ceases to struggle, I remove the trap, release the noose, and get as far away as I can before the dog regains its full faculties. I do not necessarily recommend either of these methods of releasing dogs from traps. I'm just explaining how I do it.

CATCHING FOXES AND COYOTES FOR THE LIVE MARKET

I catch canines for the live market, and of course this necessitates handling and controlling these animals without harming or killing them. I do not recommend this technique to anybody, either, because of the obvious possibility of getting bitten. But again, here's how I go about it: Before approaching the trapped animal, I get my equipment ready: a sturdy catch pole, a heavy pair of leather welder's gloves, a hardwood stick about 8 inches long and ½ to 1 inch thick, a 12-inch adjustable wrench, and a roll of duct tape with the end loosened so I can grasp it easily when the time comes.

Approaching the animal head-on, I ease the noose of the catchpole over its head and snug it down tight enough so that it won't slip off over the animal's head, but not so tight it cuts off the airflow, then secure the locking device on the cable so it can't back off. Sometimes this can be a tedious process, with the animal biting the cable and doing everything it can to avoid the noose, but eventually I get it done.

With the animal firmly under control with the catchpole, I force it to the ground on its side, with the trapped leg down. Then I stand on the pole with both feet, put on my leather gloves and kneel on the pole fairly close behind the animal's head. I then slide my hand along the catchpole behind the animal's head and firmly grasp an ear, pulling its head back so I can get the hardwood stick between its jaws.

Getting a canine to bite the stick can be surprisingly hard. Gray and red foxes are usually pretty cooperative in this regard, but often, if the animal is a subordinate coyote in the area's pecking order, it will go meek and docile at this point, submitting to whatever indignities I want to subject it to. That's what the adjustable wrench is for; sometimes I have to wedge it between the animal's jaws to get them far enough open to get the stick in.

Catching foxes and coyotes for the live market requires extra care and caution. Getting bitten by a wild canine isn't a pleasant experience.

I always make sure the stick is hooked behind both upper and lower canine teeth, and then I grasp the snout, holding the jaws firmly together. Then I shake off the other glove and grab the roll of duct tape. I make several wraps around one end of the stick, then run it across the snout to the other end and wrap it with several turns. Then I securely tape the snout, running a few wraps up to cover the animal's eyes as well. I've found they're much less jumpy and don't fight as much if they can't see.

Next I tape the back feet together, take the animal out of the trap, and tape the front feet together. Then I tape the front feet and the back feet together, and the job is done. Only then do I take my weight off the catchpole and remove the noose from the animal's neck.

As I said several paragraphs ago, I do not recommend this technique to anyone. I have never been bitten doing it this way, but I have no illusions—one of these days, it's going to happen. I treat every coyote and fox as carefully as if they were venomous snakes, but someday one of them will nail me.

I guess it'll serve me right.

Part III

WHEN YOU'RE NOT TRAPPING

17

Efficient Fur Handling and Marketing

My grandfather had a saying: "Chicken one day, feathers the next." As a kid, I didn't give it much thought, but as an adult I sure know what Granddad was talking about. For most of us, that's what life is—mostly feathers, with few chickens sprinkled in here and there.

As we all know, it happens on the trapline, too. Most days are somewhere between the extremes, and some days are pure, unadulterated feathers. But usually once or twice during every trapping season, things fall into place. The weather cooperates, the critters move, you have a lot of good sets in working order . . . and Lady Luck smiles. Trap after trap after trap holds furbearers, and before you've finished your line you're grinning like a mule eating sawbriers. (That was another of Granddad's sayings.)

The grin lasts until sometime during the drive home. That's when the other side of the coin pops up. Because the down side of catching a bunch of critters is that you then have to deal with them in the fur shed.

There was a time when many trappers didn't worry about skinning. Until the fur market crash of 1987, it seemed like you couldn't swing a dead cat without hitting a country fur buyer. Most trappers had one or more buyers within easy range, and that gave them the option of selling their catch on a daily basis "in the round"—that is, with the fur still attached to the carcass.

But following the 1987 crash and through the subsequent years of low markets and dwindling numbers of active trappers, most country buyers disappeared. Today's trappers can still find ready markets for their fur, but for most of us it's no longer as convenient as it used to be. We have to do something with it first.

Doing something with it can be as simple as skinning the day's catch and freezing the pelts until you can make a trip to the nearest fur buyer, or until a traveling buyer can come to you. But even at that, you still

The upside of being a good trapper is that you sometimes catch a lot of fur. The downside of being a good trapper is that . . . you sometimes catch a lot of fur.

have to skin it, and if you're going to skin it, you might as well finish it. Stretching and drying fur takes a little more time, but gives the trapper many more options than selling green pelts. Local buyers are still an option with finished fur, but so are state and regional fur auctions, not to mention the much larger international auctions hosted by organizations like North American Fur Auctions and Fur Harvesters Auction, Inc.

However, finished fur must be finished well. A well-prepared, properly stretched and dried fur pelt is worth considerably more than the same fur when it's green, but a poorly handled stretched and dried fur pelt will be worth far less. It's impossible to undo a poor fur handling job. Here's a step-by-step guide for getting it right.

THE PROPER SETTING

It's hard to cook a meal if you don't have a kitchen and some cooking utensils. Likewise, it's hard to put up fur if you don't have a place to work and the proper tools for the job. I've skinned hundreds of furbearers hanging from a piece of rope from a tree limb in the back yard. I still do that every once in a while when the weather is nice and I'm in the mood for it, but if you're going to handle fur you need more than a rope dangling from a shade tree.

Fur handling areas can be elaborate or simple, small or large. A portion of an attic or basement can serve nicely, but there's a certain amount of mess and odor associated with handling fur, and it's usually better to get your fur handling activities a little farther from your living quarters—in a garage, tool shed, shop, or other outbuilding.

It's important to have a dry, warm place for skinning and processing fur. Open-air skinning under a shade tree in the yard can be pleasant if the weather is mild, but it's not so much fun when it's 35 degrees, dark, and raining.

You need a place to hang animals for skinning, plus a little more room to hang wet animals so they can dry. Many trappers use commercially made or homemade skinning gambrels, but I prefer a loop of soft rope, eye-bolted to a sturdy rafter. The loop of rope is half-hitched around an animal's hind foot, and it works very well for me. Elsewhere around my shed are a dozen or so lengths of trapping tie wire attached to other eyebolts, for hanging wet animals before skinning. Two or three quick wraps around a critter's foot holds it in place while it drips and air-dries. For skinning beavers, you'll need a sturdy flat table or bench about waist high.

My fleshing beam stands in a corner when not in use, and I use it in that corner, with a plastic bucket to hold the fat, flesh, and other scrapings. Under the beam and on the floor under my skinning rope, I put down a layer of corrugated cardboard to keep the concrete floor of my fur shed from getting so greasy and bloody. I use large cardboard shipping cartons, collected during the off-season from appliance stores.

You also need a place to hang stretched pelts while they dry. Ideally, this should be out of the walkways. If your fur handling area has exposed rafters, it's a simple matter to drive a series of nails or cup hooks along

Fleshing beavers requires a little patience and a lot of elbow grease.

Handling your own fur is an added demand on your trapping time, but in many cases it's the only viable option for selling your fur. And there's something awfully satisfying about looking at a ceiling full of well-handled furs.

the rafters. If the ceiling is enclosed, drive the nails or hooks into a long 2x2, then attach it to the ceiling with screws or bolts. Put up as many hangers as you have space for. It will surprise you how many of them you're going to need.

PROPER FIELD CARE

The first step in good fur handling begins in the field. This should go without saying, but judging from the condition of the in-the-round furbearers I've seen in the vehicles and fur sheds of many of my fellow trappers, many trappers don't attach very much importance to this initial aspect of proper fur handling.

Let's talk about water animals first. Beavers and otters don't require much in the way of in-the-field care, except to avoid stacking them on top of each other so they can cool and air-dry as you finish running your line. Because of their short fur, these furbearers dry out in no time. Otter fur is susceptible to singeing, though, so it's important to keep otters from coming into contact with freezing metal or to allow them to jostle back and forth and rub against equipment or other furbearers during transportation.

Mink and muskrats, if they're wet, require a little more attention. If the fur is muddy, rinse the animal thoroughly at the catch site to remove as much mud and dirt as possible. After the dirt is washed out of the fur, lay the animal across your booted leg or on a flat, dry surface such as your truck tailgate and use the edge of your hand to squeegee excess water out of the pelt. With a wet mink, grab the animal by the head and pop it several times, then grab it by both hind feet and repeat the popping process. (Don't pop wet muskrats like this, though, or you'll break their backs and make skinning them very difficult.)

Next, roll the still-damp mink or muskrat into a double layer of old newspaper and lay it flat in the back of your vehicle. As with beavers and otters, try to avoid piling mink and 'rats on top of each other. By the time you reach home and start skinning, all but the most waterlogged specimens will be dry and fluffy. (Be sure to keep dry mink and muskrats away from the wet ones.)

Rolling wet mink, muskrats, and other small furbearers in old newspaper as soon as they're removed from the trap helps dry the fur quickly.

Wet possums and coons are tougher. If one of these animals is muddy, and they often are, wash it thoroughly, even if it results in a wetter animal than you started with. The mud has to come out eventually, and it's easier to get out when it's wet.

Coons and possums are stockier and larger than mink, so it's harder to pop them to get rid of excess water. But it's not impossible, and you can sling a lot of water out of the fur this way. Using your hand to squeegee the animal also helps. But even after popping and squeegeeing, the animal will be too wet to get dry by rolling it in newspaper. Instead, if possible, lay the animals so they don't touch in your vehicle and let them air-dry as you finish your run.

For predators such as fox, coyote, and bobcat—and dry-land coons and possums as well, incidentally—the most important thing is to avoid getting blood on the pelt and to allow the furbearer to cool as quickly as possible after being killed. If you dispatch trapped upland furbearers by shooting them in the head, try to hold the animal up by a hind foot while it bleeds out. When you put the animal in your truck, wrap its head in several layers of newspaper or old rags to absorb the blood and keep it from soaking into the fur.

PRE-SKINNING TREATMENT IN THE FUR SHED

As soon as you get home, take the day's catch to your skinning area. Hang any still-wet coons and possums by a front foot, so the water can run down the guard hairs and drip off. Remove the wet newspaper from your 'rats and mink and lay them belly down on flat cardboard on the floor. If any are still exceptionally wet, re-wrap them with fresh newspaper. Lay beavers and otters belly-down on the cardboard, along with any dry coons, possums, or predators. Laying the animals belly down retards spoilage if the floor is cool. Next, turn on a fan to move the air around, and if it's below freezing, get a little bit of heat going as well. Not too much heat, though, or you'll run the risk of spoilage. Now is a good time to take a break and rest a bit or grab a bite to eat while any wet fur continues to dry.

SKINNING

Sharp knives of the proper size and shape are essential for efficient skinning, but other tools are important as well. A butcher's sharpening steel is a valuable accessory in any skinning shed, as are poultry shears, plenty of shop rags or towels, a plastic or rubber skinning apron, and a box or two of latex or nitrile disposable gloves. Not only are the gloves handy in helping keep your hands cleaner, they also help protect the skinner from disease. *Never* skin furbearers without using these gloves.

Be sure you have the proper tools to do a quality skinning and fleshing job.

With the exception of beaver, almost all modern-day buyers want case-skinned furs. In case-skinning, a cut is made from heel to heel and the pelt is peeled from the animal's body from back to front, taking if off the carcass like a sock without splitting the belly of the pelt. Beavers are skinned "open," by splitting the belly of the pelt from chin to tail and working the pelt off the carcass around the sides.

There are as many techniques of case-skinning a furbearer as there are trappers who skin them, but the following is an efficient method: Hang the animal from one hind foot at about shoulder height or slightly higher. Using a sharp knife, ring all four feet at the ankles and wrists. If the animal being skinned is a muskrat or nutria, ring the tail at this time, too, cutting through the skin at the hairline.

Grasp the loose hind foot, pull it away from the other foot until the legs and skin are tight, and cut along the back of the legs from one ankle to the other. With most furbearers, the connecting straight-across cut will pass just in front of the vent.

Cut around the sides of the vent to the base of the tail and split the skin for about a third of the way on the underside of the tail. Using your knife to get things started and your fingers to pull the hide, work the skin away from the tailbone and off the back legs. Pull the tailbone the rest of the way out of the tail skin, using a homemade or commercially made tail-pulling tool (shown at upper right in above photo).

Continue to work the hide off the rear legs and then pull the pelt down over the body, turning it inside out as you go. As the front legs come into view, pull them free from the pelt, turning the front-leg portion of the pelt inside out as well. Continue pulling the pelt down over the neck (some careful cutting may be necessary here on canines and cats) until the ear butts show. Carefully cut through the cartilage at the base of each ear. Pull the pelt a little more and the edges of the eyes will become visible. Cut the pelt very carefully to free the eyeholes, being careful not to make the holes any larger than they already are. Pull again, and the pelt will come loose to the corners of the mouth. Make another careful cut on each side, cut off the bottom-lip portion of the pelt, and skin the rest of the head out all the way to the tip of the nose.

Beavers are skinned "open." Lay the beaver belly up on a flat, sturdy work surface. Ring all four feet and the tail at the hairline, or use heavy shears, loppers, or a hatchet to cut off the feet and the tail. With a sharp, thin-bladed knife, make a single incision along the midline of the belly, from the chin all the way to the tail, cutting carefully around each side of the vent. Next, switch to a curve-bladed knife and start peeling the pelt back from both sides of the midline cut, working around to the back of

Don't get in too big a hurry when skinning, especially around the head. Take the time to make precise cuts and keep the earholes and eyeholes small, and your pelts will receive better consideration on the auction table.

the animal. Continue cutting and pulling the pelt until the tail section is free, and work the legs free of the pelt as you come to them. When the pelt is cut loose from everything but the beaver's neck and head, throw the whole pelt back over the head and allow its weight to help keep the pelt tight as you use the knife to cut the skin loose from the head. Follow the same procedure for skinning the ears, eyes and lips as outlined above, and skin the pelt all the way down to the tip of the nose.

DEVELOP YOUR OWN SYSTEM

If your skinning chores include more than one animal of the same species, things will go faster if you proceed in assembly-line fashion. For example, ring all the feet and tails, then move on to the next step. Even if you're dealing with a number of different species, doing all the foot ringing at the same time is usually a time-saver.

It's usually best to skin the driest animals first, since this gives the wetter ones a little more time to dry. However, there's an important exception: otters should *not* be skinned dry, because their fur is very susceptible to singeing. If an otter is completely dry when you start to skin it, sprinkle a little water on the pelt.

For other furbearers, drier is better, but don't leave animals unskinned just because they're not completely dry. There's a better way to handle the situation. I prefer to start with dry coyotes or cats, then dry coons or possums, and finish up with dry mink and muskrats. Then I'll reverse the order, skinning the wetter mink and 'rats first, and finishing up with the wet longhaired critters. As soon as I skin each wet animal, I stop working long enough to pop the pelt vigorously a few times and pull it fur side out onto an appropriately sized wire stretcher. Then I hang the stretcher in front of my fur-shed fan. When I finish skinning the wet longhaired fur, I skin my beavers and otters.

Skinning a varied catch of furbearers in this order allows the maximum time possible for wet pelts to dry, and minimizes the mildew and spoilage problems associated with wet fur.

FLESHING

As with skinning, fleshing goes quicker if you develop a system and stick with it. It's best to start with the dry pelts, once again because this provides extra drying time for the wet ones. Here's my personal system: I start with the mink, using a 12-inch double-handled drawknife and a homemade fleshing beam made from a 36-inch piece of 1x4, shaped like a male mink board but thicker and sturdier. For my money, it's the perfect board for fleshing mink and muskrats.

Fleshing mink and muskrats is easy and requires only a minute or so per pelt.

Both mink and muskrats are easy to flesh. Mink first: Start by pulling the pelt onto the board so that the belly and back are on the edges of the board, and the sides of the animal are on the board's wide surfaces. Beginning around the ears and lips, carefully scrape the loose fat and flesh away from the hide, working down toward the front legs but stopping just before you reach them. Now, flip the board over and scrape the other side of the head. You don't have to move the pelt on the board; just flip the board.

When you reach the front leg on this side, move the pelt up the board so that the leg is over the rounded end of the board and the belly is mostly on your side of the board. Begin scraping where you see the little glob of fat under the front leg, and continue down the belly side of the pelt, scraping off the fat that's usually present on the lower belly. Position the other front leg on the point of the board and scrape it the same way, getting the other side of the belly in the process. Leave the red saddle of flesh on the back of the mink pelt; most buyers prefer it that way. After you've learned how to do it, this whole process won't take 90 seconds.

Muskrats are fleshed on the same mink stretcher-shaped board, and they're even easier than mink. Put the pelt on the stretcher with the back of the pelt facing you, and make a couple light swipes down the entire length of the pelt to remove any loose flesh or fat. Stop right there; the back is now clean enough. Turn the board over and scrape away the loose flesh on the belly side, being sure to get the stuff in the armpit area of the pelt. Don't scrape too close on this side, either. Just getting the gobs of stuff off is good enough.

Next on the agenda are the dry longhaired pelts—cats, coyotes, foxes, coons, and possums. I switch to a larger, longer fleshing beam for these bigger animals, but stay with the 12-inch, two-handled fleshing knife. Possums are easier than coons, so I usually do them first.

The drill is much the same as with mink and muskrats, except the scale is a little larger. Possums are usually very fat, but again, you don't want to scrape them too closely. Do so and you run the risk of either tearing the skin or damaging the guard hairs. Just take off the big gobs of fat and meat, working the pelt around the beam so you can reach every part of it.

Coons are tougher, and they require more elbow grease. The process is the same, though: Start around the ears and lips on each side, work down to the neck and shoulder area, then move the pelt so the front leg holes are over the end of the beam and carefully scrape the fat and flesh away. Remove the saddle on coons, and scrape them as clean as you can get them. Pay special attention to the gristly stuff on the neck of a coon pelt, high between the shoulders. This tough area often requires some heavy labor.

Bobcats, foxes, and coyotes usually don't need much scraping, but occasionally you'll find a little fat under the armpits or, more commonly, on the lower belly—especially on cats. A few light passes with the two-handled knife are usually enough to clean this up. Scrape cats and foxes lightly and carefully, though, because their skin is thin and papery and tears easily.

Fleshing beavers and otters involves little finesse, but a lot of hard work. Just remember, the cleaner the better. Pay special attention to the tail and lower belly of an otter. The fat and gristle in the tail are tough as leather, and the belly will easily taint if it's not fully cleaned. Again, as when skinning them, otter pelts are prone to singe when being fleshed, so be sure the fur is damp when you pull it onto the fleshing beam. If it's already dry, dampen it with a few sprinkles of water.

After all the dry pelts are finished, go back and flesh any remaining wet pelts, in whatever order you prefer. When the wet ones are fully fleshed, put them back on the wire stretchers fur-side out and hang them up overnight. They'll finish drying in that length of time, and you can stretch them the following day.

THE STRETCHING PROCESS

Stretching your furs is the easiest part of the whole process, and a good thing, too, because by the time you're ready to stretch your furs, you'll also probably be ready to go in the house and hit the sack. There are basically just two things to remember: first, stretch pelts firmly but don't over-stretch them; and second, you can use wire for everything but mink and otters. Coons also look a little better when stretched on wood, but wire stretchers are acceptable.

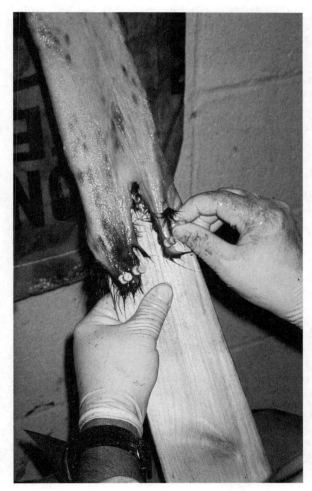

Stretch your pelts firmly, but don't over-stretch them. Wooden stretchers are better for otters, mink, and coons, but all other fur-bearers can be stretched on wood or wire.

To stretch a coon, possum, fox, muskrat, or other critter on wire, pull the pelt on the stretcher fur side in and center the belly and back on opposite sides. Starting with the belly side, fasten the back legs with the metal fur hook and pull it down until the pelt is smooth and firm. Turn the frame over and fasten the back of the pelt at the base of the tail, pulling the hook until the pelt is firm as well. For coons and possums, turn the frame back to the belly side and cut away the loose pouch of skin on the lower belly.

After about twenty-four hours, take cat, coyote, and red fox pelts off the stretchers, turn them fur side out, and put them back on the stretchers to finish drying. Leave the other species (including gray fox) skin side out.

At least two sizes of boards are needed for mink, one for males and one for females. Years ago, I used a third, slightly larger size for extra-large males, but found they didn't bring any more money than the other males, so I abandoned the effort.

Center the pelt on the board as described above. Starting on the belly side, put a couple push pins in each of the legs, pulling them firm but not too tight. On the back, start by putting a temporary pin in the middle of the tail where it joins the body. Then, working from one side of the tail to the other, tack the tail out flat and as wide as possible, putting the pins a half-inch to an inch apart. Finish the tacking process by pulling the edge of the skin at the back of the legs toward the tail and pinning it there. Trim away the fringe of loose skin around the belly, put a wooden wedge between the board and the belly of the pelt, and you're done. The process is the same for coons and otters, except, of course, the board is much bigger and the coon's tails are not tacked down. (If you don't have any otter boards, you can use a number 6 stretcher for the body and tack the tail flat on an XL mink board or a 1x6, but this is a poor substitute for having the right stretchers.)

STRETCHING BEAVER PELTS

Beavers are a little more trouble to put up than other furs. There are two basic methods: lacing the pelt inside an adjustable metal hoop, or tacking the pelt to a large flat board such as a half-sheet of plywood.

If you use the hoop method, you'll need a spool of cheap nylon string and a bagging needle. Start at the nose of the beaver, lacing the string through the edge of the pelt and around the hoop at one-inch to two-inch intervals, working your way all the way around the circle and back to the starting point. To keep from having to pull so much string through the holes, it's helpful to cut the string and tie it off about a quarter of the way

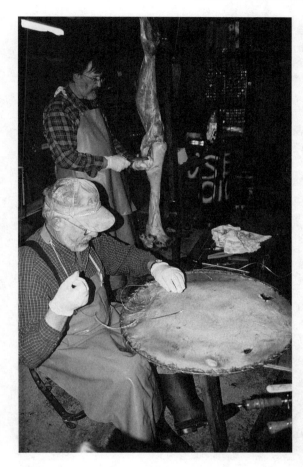

Beaver pelts can be sewn into a hoop or tacked onto a plywood board. Both require a little patience.

around the circle, then start fresh with a new length of string. When the pelt is fully laced into the hoop, loosen the sliding setscrews and enlarge the size of the hoop enough to tighten the pelt inside the hoop.

If you're tacking the pelt to a board, lay the pelt flesh side up on the board and start by driving a two-inch finishing nail at the nose and the center of the tail butt, then putting two more nails at the sides, so the four nails are in the shape of a cross. Now, start splitting the distance between nails, putting four more in so there are now eight nails spaced equally around the sides of the pelt. Keep on doing this, splitting the distance between nails each time—sixteen nails, then thirty-two, and so on—until the nails are about one to two inches apart around the edge of the pelt. Now raise the pelt up on the nails all the way around the edges, so that the green hide is away from the board so air can circulate underneath. Lean the board against a wall or hang it from a rafter to allow the pelt to dry. Some trappers cut a 24-inch diameter hole out of the center of their beaver boards to allow for better air circulation and better drying. If you elect to do this, there's no need to raise the pelt on the nails after tacking it down.

Whether you use boards or hoops for your beavers, the stretched green pelt should be pulled just tight enough so that all the wrinkles are removed and the skin doesn't sag when hung up to dry. If the green hide feels like a drumhead, it's too tight.

MARKETING OPTIONS

There is no "best" option for marketing fur. Some trappers, as already mentioned, live close enough to raw fur buyers that they can either sell their catch "in the round" every day. Many other trappers skin their catch and freeze the green pelts and sell them in batches throughout the season, either carrying the pelts to a buyer or arranging for the buyer to come pick them up.

Fur sales hosted by state trappers associations are excellent outlets for both green and finished fur, and offer the added advantage of allowing trappers to inspect each other's fur handling techniques and trade trapping stories.

Both these selling options save the trapper the time and effort of fleshing and stretching. Another plus for many trappers is that selling to local buyers provides for a quicker payoff because the seller doesn't have to wait for his money.

Selling fur at local or regional fur auctions, which are usually sponsored by state trappers associations, is the preferred choice of many trappers. Most of these auctions handle both green and finished fur, and often the green stuff goes for as much as (sometimes more than) finished pelts. There's a commission on all sales, usually 4 or 5 percent, but the increase in prices paid usually more than offsets it.

One obvious advantage of selling at auction is the competition factor between buyers; trappers are more likely to get good prices for their furs, especially well-handled finished fur. Another advantage is that attending these sales allows trappers to inspect other trappers' collections of both green and finished fur, and see firsthand the better prices paid for high-quality merchandise. Fur auctions also provide a forum for trappers to exchange ideas and techniques on both trapping and fur handling. Beginning and intermediate trappers will find these gatherings very instructional, and even veteran steel-handlers can always learn a trick or two.

Finally, there are the large Canadian auction houses, which is where all the country-bought fur winds up eventually. Many trappers who finish their fur ship directly to these companies and market their fur this way.

The advantage is obvious: by going directly to the final seller of the raw product, the trapper eliminates several middlemen from the food chain. However, the seller has to wait longer for his fur, and if some of the pelts don't sell (a common occurrence, especially in times of uncertain markets), the seller's money is tied up for an undetermined time period.

So, in the end, the "best" selling option depends largely on the circumstances and preferences of each individual trapper. For most of us, a combination of selling strategies works best—selling part of our catch at local auction or to local buyers, shipping part of it to a large auction house, perhaps even selling some green fur when time is tight and the trapline is long.

IS FINISHING FUR WORTH THE BOTHER?

When furs are stretched and dried properly, they're almost always more valuable than raw pelts. And, as we've already mentioned, putting up your fur unquestionably gives a trapper more options when it's time to

Yes, it's worth the bother.

sell. And unless you ship to one of the Canadian auction houses mentioned above, you could still, in the end, say "no sale" and walk away with your fur. After all, it's stretched and dried and, for the short term at least, resistant to spoilage as long as it's stored properly.

The downside of putting up fur, of course, is that it requires more work. Taking a pickup truck full of fur from the "in the round" stage to a rafter full of fleshed, stretched, and dried furs requires no small investment of time and energy. Whether it's worth it or not is up to the individual trapper.

But I can tell you this: when I walk into my fur shed toward the end of the season and look up at those rows of well-handled mink, coons, muskrats, otters, beavers, gray foxes, coyotes, red foxes, and miscellaneous other critters, it gives me a feeling like no other. I tend to forget about all the hours those hanging pelts represent, and I catch myself just standing there among those pelts and looking at them. During these times, I feel that yes, it's worth all the bother.

18

Post-Season Chores

The end of trapping season doesn't signal an end to your trapping-related chores. In addition to putting up the last few days' worth of fur, there's also quite a bit of cleaning and fix-up work to do. Your trapping equipment represents a substantial investment, and the sooner you clean your traps, vehicles, and other hardware, the longer they'll last and the more efficiently they'll work next season. Unused baits, lures, and urines need prompt attention as well to keep them in good shape and usable the following season.

Anyone who's ever tried it is well aware that it's difficult to keep a trapline sailing along smoothly and efficiently throughout an entire season. It's even harder to keep right on working after the season closes and pull all that needed maintenance on your equipment. You're tired from the rigors of a long season, the anticipation and excitement of checking your sets is no longer there to keep you pushing, and you feel like you've earned some serious couch time.

All those things may be true, but they don't change the fact that there's a pile of dirty traps on the floor in the fur shed, and your hip boots have a leak, and your trapline vehicle needs a new set of shocks and looks like somebody just pulled it out of a mud pit. Those things are going to have to be dealt with eventually, so you might as well get them out of the way.

Proper post-season equipment care begins when you start pulling your traps. Do this chore right, and you can avoid a lot of trouble later. Before I figured this out, I built myself a heck of a catastrophe at the end of every trapping season.

By season's end, I usually have between 250 and 300 traps out if I'm water trapping, and somewhere between 70 and 100 if I'm working the high country. When I was younger and had more steam, the totals were even higher. Before I learned better, I'd leave my entire trapline in place until the very end. Then I'd get up extra early on the last day and tear

It's difficult to keep a trapline going smoothly through the duration of the season. And when it's over, it's still not over.

around my line like my hair was on fire, trying to pull everything in one check. I'd leap out of the truck at each stop, grab all the traps at a trot, remove any catches and throw the whole mess—traps, stakes, grapples, wire, grass, mud, trapped animal, and all—into the bed of my truck and speed off to the next stop.

By the end of the day, my old truck bed would be mounded up with the messiest-looking pile of tangled steel you ever saw, and I'd be worn to a frazzle. The only way I could get that tangled mass of muddy steel out of the truck was drop the tailgate and start pulling and tugging on whatever part of the pile I could get a grip on. After several minutes of straining, it would finally roll ponderously out onto the ground, and I ran a good risk of getting buried under it. Hard as it was, getting that mass of traps out of the truck was the easy part. Then I had to untangle and sort them. And if you think there's any enjoyment in that at all, think again.

LESSON LEARNED

Nowadays, I pull my line over a span of at least two days at the end of the season. Sometimes three days, if I have a lot of traps out. This gives me enough time to dismantle things a little as I go, and organize the pile of equipment in the back of my truck.

Before the first pulling day, empty your vehicle of the clutter that inevitably accumulates during a trapping season. If you plan to make a few new sets or remakes at new or hot locations, carry only enough equipment to take care of those anticipated sets and remakes, but get rid of the rest of it—traps, stakes, drags, baits and lures, that sort of stuff. Then put in as many empty plastic totes (or whatever you use for trap storage containers) as your vehicle will comfortably hold. I also throw in one large wooden box for trap stakes and two five gallon buckets, one for snares and one for scrap trapping wire.

As you pull each water set, swish it around in the water to remove excess mud while it's still wet and easier to get off the steel. When you pull a dry set, knock the trap against your boot or against the ground, or set it and spring it a time or two so the dirt is knocked free.

After you've pulled all the traps at a stop, carry them to the truck and conduct a brief work session, removing the tie wire and saving or discarding the stakes, depending on what kind of stake it is and what kind of shape it's in. The trap goes in a tote with others of its kind, the stake goes in the wooden box, the wire goes in a bucket—and the mess is kept under control.

When you're pulling up at the end of the season, take a few extra seconds to clean the mud and dirt off your traps while it's still wet. It'll save you a lot of headaches later.

On this first pulling day, I'm pretty selective about which stops I pull. Generally, my goal is to leave the best, most productive, freshest stops for the final day, to increase as much as possible my odds of catching more fur. However, don't pull some of the traps at a stop and leave others; doing so is confusing and time-consuming. If you decide to pull traps at a particular stop, pull them all, so you won't have to stop at that place the next day. When you finish the run that day, unload your vehicle of all traps and equipment and replace the full containers and buckets with empty ones.

Granted, pulling your line this way takes a little longer, and it probably will cost you a pelt or two from the sets pulled that first day. But you won't be so worn out when you wrap things up that final afternoon, and you'll gain back the time—and more—because the post-season clean-up and straighten-up will go faster.

NOT THROUGH YET

The next post-season chore is to clean and sort your traps and other equipment, and either repair or set aside for repair any traps or hardware that need attention. As mentioned at the beginning of this chapter, this is a chore best done sooner rather than later. I confess that I usually take a week or so off after the season closes, and during that week or so I do my best not to think about trapping at all.

But sometime before spring, I'm out there in the fur shed, cleaning and repairing my traps. If any of my traps are still caked with dirt and mud, they're set aside for a trip to the car wash and the high-pressure wand.

Usually, though, I do a good enough job of washing off my water traps (all my 1, 1½, and 2 coilsprings, 2 longsprings, large beaver and otter footholds, and the few guard-style longspring traps I use for muskrats) that they only need a lick or two with a wire brush and they're ready for waxing. My dry-land traps (1¾ coilsprings mostly, plus a few 3 coilsprings) usually don't need any more cleaning than do the water traps, but I boil them before waxing them to help deodorize them a little more.

At the same time I'm wire brushing the traps, I inspect the dog and pan notch, touching the edges up with a file to re-square the contact surfaces and knock off any burs, rust, or rough spots that might have developed during the season.

Depending on how many traps I used during the season and how diligently I work at it, I can usually get these cleaning, filing, and sorting

Before boiling or waxing traps for the next season's use, clean any remaining dirt off with a wire brush. Use a large brush for fast work, and a smaller one to get into the hard-to-reach places.

chores done in two days, dealing with 300 traps or more. As I'm going through them, I set aside any traps that need more extensive repairs such as new springs, a new pan, a new trigger, or whatever. When I'm done with the cleaning, I go through the repair pile and make a list of the parts I'll need and get them ordered right away. I want to have the parts in hand so I can take advantage of odd free time to do the work—and also so I don't forget to order them and get caught short when the next season rolls around.

Next, I again try to forget about trapping-related things for a while, because by this time spring is approaching and it's time to hunt turkeys. Following the spring turkey season, and before summer arrives with a vengeance, I wax my water-set foothold traps, boil and then wax my dry-set foothold traps and either cold-dip or spray-paint my body-grippers. If I get a timely start and don't goof off much, I can get my entire string of traps done in one day, using two propane cookers so I can wax and boil traps at the same time. And since this trap treatment stuff is messy work, I try to get it all done in one day.

After the footholds are cool and the wax has hardened, I store the traps in airtight containers in the coolest part of my fur shed, along with a couple handfuls of cedar shavings or pine needles. The cold-dipped body-grippers are hung up and aired out for a week or so to give the petroleum odor time to dissipate. Then I hang them from the rafters in the fur shed, overhead and out of the way.

OTHER EQUIPMENT THAT NEEDS ATTENTION

Your fur shed, if it's like mine, will be a holy mess by the end of the season. As mentioned in the fur-handling chapter, I cover the floor of my skinning and fleshing area with flattened cardboard packing crates. This greatly simplifies the clean-up process. After the season, I remove the bloody, greasy cardboard and replace it with fresh stuff.

Clean your wire and wooden stretchers, too. Wipe them down with a clean rag dampened with a weak ammonia solution. This cuts grease and retards mildew. The easiest way to clean your fleshing tools and skinning knives is to run them through the dishwasher, but try to do this when the lady of the house isn't around.

However you clean them, sharpen and oil them afterwards, and either wrap them in an oily rag or store them in an airtight plastic container in the fur shed. Few things are more aggravating than finding your collection of fur-handling blades pitted and rusted two days before the season starts.

Don't neglect your fur-handling equipment during the off season. Wiping down your wire stretchers with an oily rag keeps them from rusting.

Give your digging tools, sifters, and other trapline hardware a good cleaning as well, but of course don't oil digging tools and sifters because of potential odor problems. Don't forget to see to your waders, boots, gloves, and other equipment.

Finally, sit down with a pad and pencil and either mentally or physically take inventory of your equipment. Try to anticipate your needs for the coming year and make a detailed list of what you think you're going to need. Be sure to order these supplies well in advance of the coming season. Summer and fall trappers' conventions are excellent places to pick up supplies; prices are generally favorable, you'll save shipping costs, and you can also compare prices between dealers.

Don't forget about that off-season bait-gathering chore. The heads from fish caught in June and July make excellent coon bait in November and December.

Between the time you make next year's supply list and the time you go to a trappers' convention to buy those supplies, you'll probably hear a rumor that the fish are biting somewhere. And, since you got to work during the post-season and handled your maintenance chores in timely fashion, you'll probably have enough leisure time to go see if the rumor is true.

But wait. When you go fishing and catch a big mess of bluegills or crappies or catfish, and you bring them home and clean them, don't throw away all that perfectly good coon bait. Put the heads and guts in plastic bags, ice cream buckets, or coffee cans and store them in the freezer. Come November, they'll come in handy.

A trapper's work is never completely done.

19

Trappers' Conventions and Other Learning Opportunities

Most trappers aren't hermits, but we like to get out into the backcountry and do our thing—going one on one with our target animals, reading sign, trying to think like the critters we're trying to catch, and using our wits and abilities to be as successful as possible.

The fact that the backcountry, for most of us, is usually a farm or two, or maybe a creek or river that flows within sight and sound of homes and highways, isn't important. What's important is that we're out there alone, or maybe with a trusted partner, friend, or family member, soaking up what a buddy of mine likes to call "the noisy silence" of nature. We're out there precisely because it's the Out There, and it provides what we need—a temporary escape from the hustle and bustle of humanity.

Contrast this attitude with that of the suit-and-tie businessman. He wants to succeed, just like we do. (No matter what a trapper says about just wanting to enjoy nature, he still wants to catch some fur.) But while the trapper avoids crowds, the banker or the insurance executive seeks them out. Traditional businessmen network. They interact and interface and interchange ideas and strategies. By contrast, trappers go their own way and want others to return the favor.

See the problem? The same personality traits that make us trappers in the first place work against us becoming better at it. We don't seek each other out. We avoid each other. On the trapline, this is fine. Less direct competition with other trappers usually makes for a better overall experience. But during those long months when trapping season is closed, there's no need to avoid each other. Yet many trappers still do. The same lone-wolf attitude that drives us to the trapline in the first place makes us shy away from gatherings, even when they're gatherings of trappers.

It's a serious mistake. Trappers' conventions, whether local, state, or national, are mother lodes of expertise and information, and to cash in all

State, regional, and national trappers' conventions are packed with learning opportunities for beginners and veteran trappers alike. Equipment, knowledge, and friendships are all there waiting.

Almost all trappers' conventions, small and large, include seminars given by accomplished trappers.

you have to do is show up. No matter how good you are, there's always something new to learn.

A trappers' convention provides the opportunity to really dig into the subject with other like-minded people, both in organized seminars by experienced trappers and in conversations with other trappers. You'll find others who've had the same problems you've had. You'll soak up more usable information in a few days at a convention than in ten years on the trapline by yourself.

Conventions are the best place to stock up on supplies for the coming season, at competitive prices. Conventions give you the opportunity to handle new or unfamiliar equipment before making purchases—something that's not possible when ordering from a catalog.

Conventions, of course, aren't the only way to plug into the information stream available to modern-day trappers. Fifty years ago, good trapline information was hard to come by. Then, only one trapping-related magazine existed (*Hunter-Trader-Trapper*, which became *Fur-Fish-Game* and continues to provide trappers with good information), and the few trapping books available back then were repetitive, redundant, mostly poorly written, and full of bad advice.

Today, there are several magazines devoted to trapping, and traditional hunting magazines print trapline-related articles from time to time. There are literally hundreds of books available on all aspects of trapping, and though some are still poorly written and contain bad advice, most are valuable learning tools. In addition, there are scores of trapping videos and DVDs on the market, and while some of these are poorly done and don't yield much information, others are of extremely high quality and instructional value.

Many accomplished trappers offer personal, one-on-one trapline instructions, either on the instructor's or the student's trapline. For serious students of trapping who want to climb the learning curve quickly, there's no better way to acquire information. Of course, personal instruction is initially more expensive, but it provides the opportunity for hands-on training and is more economical in the long run because it's more efficient and provides quicker results.

The point of this chapter should be obvious by now: the wealth of information available to trappers today is staggering, and it's readily available in a wide variety of formats. Anyone interested in learning more about trapping has no excuse for not doing so.

TIPS FOR GETTING THE MOST
OUT OF A TRAPPERS' CONVENTION

1. Learn everything you can about the convention ahead of time—schedules, seminars, and other attractions in the convention area. That way, you won't miss out on something just because you weren't aware of it.

2. Include clothing for both wet and dry weather, including a light windbreaker-type jacket. Take a hat and sunscreen, and wear comfortable footwear because you'll be on your feet a lot. Good running shoes are hard to beat. A packbasket, duffel bag, or gym bag will be handy to carry catalogs, literature, and smaller purchases.

3. Make a list ahead of time of the things you want to do and see, and note the specific times of scheduled events in which you're interested. For things that don't have a specific time (such as talking with a specific manufacturer, trapper, or lure dealer), develop a priority list. If you run out of time before you get to the end of your list, at least the most important items will get taken care of.

4. Make a shopping list before you go. In the peace and quiet of home, you can realistically assess your inventory and figure out what you really need for next year. Then, when you get to the convention, stick pretty much to your list. You'll see things you want that aren't listed, and it's okay to buy some of them, but take my word for it: your eyes will bug

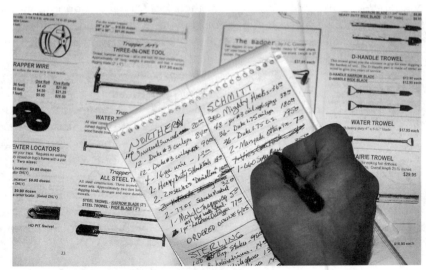

Make a shopping list before you go.

out like a grasshopper's when you see all the equipment at the dealer booths. It's easy to let your spending urges overload your trapline budget.

5. Before you start buying, make a leisurely tour of the dealers, both inside and outside the buildings. You'll be surprised how much difference there is in pricing on the same items between dealers.

6. Attend the convention's fund-raising auction (they all have one), but keep your wits about you there, too. It's easy to get caught up in the excitement and pay far too much money for an item. If you're doing that to benefit the organization, that's fine and commendable. But do it because you want to help, not because you got carried away. Keep a clear head, and make sure you can live with your decision afterward when you bid $15 for that $4.00 bottle of fox lure.

7. In general, it's best to hold off on most of your purchases until just before you're ready to leave the convention. Not only does it keep you from having to lug them around all day, but it also helps prevent breakage or damage to things like lures, videos, and books. But don't wait too long before buying, because the stuff you want may all be gone.

8. Ask about discounts, especially if you're buying a large quantity of something. Many dealers will . . . well . . . deal. Don't expect too much of a break, though, and don't be offended if the dealer says no. It doesn't cost anything to ask.

9. Bring your family, and combine the trip with a vacation. There's something fun to do nearby, no matter where the convention is being held, or somewhere along the route between the convention and your home.

10. Even at the convention itself, there's plenty for a family to do. Every trappers' convention is family-friendly, and youth attendance is especially encouraged. However, if you take your family, remember that they're probably not going to be quite as enraptured by the smell of coyote urine as you are. A pile of used 1½ coilsprings is a beautiful sight to a dedicated trapper, but it's just a pile of rusty metal to anyone else.

11. If the family's not coming, team up with a buddy or two to save on travel expenses and share the driving. Get the details straight beforehand, though; hard feelings will erupt if you want to stay four days but your buddy wants to leave after one.

12. Stay on the convention grounds if you can, either camping in a tent or in a camper. After hours is when many of the really good bull sessions take

TIPS FOR GETTING THE MOST
OUT OF A TRAPPERS' CONVENTION *continued*

place, around campfires in lawn chairs. If you're twenty miles away in
a motel, you'll miss it.

13. Don't be hesitant to ask other trappers, famous or not, about anything you want to regarding trapping or fur handling. Likewise, share
what you know. That's what a convention is for—sharing knowledge.

14. Don't be shy about talking to your heroes in the trapping industry.
They're just people, like you, and they love to talk trapping as much
as you do. However, try not to monopolize their time, especially at
their dealer booths when potential customers are there. Try to catch
them when things are slow; they'll appreciate it, and you'll get more
of their attention.

*Many of the best learning opportunities at trappers' conventions
occur after hours, in the bull sessions and unrehearsed conversations that invariably take place in the campground.*

Afterword

Please keep two things in mind here: First, the techniques and ideas covered in this book barely scratch the surface of this complex, wonderful, confusing outdoor activity we call trapping. Second, all the things in here are the opinions and techniques of a single trapper. There are many more ways to do things than the ones outlined in these pages, some of them dovetailing with what's been written here and some of them very different.

You probably noticed, for example, that there's very little mention in this book about snow and ice trapping. Nor is there any mention of the furbearers that inhabit areas of the country where deep winter snow is the norm—marten, fisher, wolverine, wolf, lynx, and ermine.

Those things are omitted for a very good reason: I know next to nothing about them. Snow trapping or trapping these deep-snow furbearers is as alien to me as Japanese algebra, because I've never done any of it. To a son of the South like me, those deep-snow, high-country furbearers are as exotic as unicorns.

However, dealing with the multi-faceted problems of the trapline for nearly five decades has taught me things about furbearer behavior and how to learn from my own experiences, good and bad. That half-century has also given me confidence. I'll never do it, but I'm absolutely certain I could go to the snowy north and in a short time I could be putting together decent catches of these species. Not the kind of catches someone who's done it all his life would put up, but I'd do okay.

I have that confidence because I've been a student of wildlife behavior and habits all my life. Which is to say, I've been a reader of sign all that time. That's how a trapper makes his wages—by being observant and learning to interpret the signs animals leave behind as they go about their everyday business of staying alive. The observant trapper is the thinking trapper, and the thinking trapper is the successful trapper.

The thing is, though, success means different things to different people. It's important for the part-time trapper to keep that in mind. When a part-time hobby trapper sees the wall of fur a full-time trapper puts up in a season, it's easy for him to get discouraged and feel inferior.

If you're a part-timer, don't feel that way. Keep things in perspective. Part-time or hobby trappers are the backbone of this industry, and the amount of fur produced by those men, women, and students who only have time to run one or two dozen traps before work or school far outweighs the fur produced by full-time, so-called "professional" trappers. The pro's season catch is higher mostly because he traps longer and with more sets, not because he's that much better than everybody else.

Sure, the longline trapper probably knows his stuff. At the current price of traps, equipment, and gasoline, he'd darn well better know his stuff or he'll be out of business pretty quick. But many part-time hobby trappers are every bit as good as most of the pros, if you look at their yield on a critters-per-trap basis.

Most trappers want to be as good as they can be, because that's just the way humans are. Obviously, that's why you're reading this book. Basketball players want to win, and so do bowlers and golfers and canasta players. Nobody ever sat down at a Las Vegas blackjack table and thought, "Boy, I sure hope I lose my shirt tonight."

Reading books like this one, and attending seminars at trapping conventions, and reading trapping magazines, and watching trapping videos, and experimenting on your own when you're out there on the trapline, will all make you a better trapper, no matter the size of your trapline. But keep in mind while you're striving to improve your trapping skills that, in the final analysis, what you're out there for is to have fun.

Yes, trapping can pay its own way, and then some. It's always nice if there's some money left over at the end of the expenses. But if your only yardstick for measuring wealth is the dollar, then here's my advice: Sell all your equipment right now, including this book, for whatever you can get for it. Forget about trapping. It's not for you. Because it's the lifestyle itself that's the biggest part of the paycheck.

I caught my first furbearer on a crisp winter morning a long time ago—a big opossum that peered out at me from a honeysuckle thicket where I'd made a crude cubby set baited with a chicken neck. That possum set my twelve-year-old heart racing like it had never raced before. This last trapping season, the final furbearer I caught was a coyote. When I first saw him flipping and bucking at my set, my heart raced exactly as it did that frosty morning in 1959. In the almost half-century between those two catches, my heart has done that same little dance literally thousands of times.

As far as I'm concerned, that makes me a rich man.

Index